# Seventy Years of Struggle and Achievement

Life Stories of Ethnic Minority Women Living in Wales

Edited and Selected by Kirsten Lavine, Meena Upadhyaya and Chris Weedon

Foreword by Julie Morgan and Jane Hutt

Introduction by Professor Terry Threadgold

Parthian, Cardigan SA43 1ED
www.parthianbooks.com
ISBN: 978-1-913640-94-1
First published in 2021 © the contributors
Edited and selected by Kirsten Lavine,
Meena Upadhyaya and Chris Weedon
Cover design by Nazma Ali
Typeset by Elaine Sharples www.typesetter.org.uk
Printed by Gomer Press, Llandysul, Wales
Parthian works with the financial support of the Books Council of Wales.

# Acknowledgements

We thank Heritage Lottery Fund (HLF) for funding this project, and the support of Beth Williams (HLF) is much appreciated. My sincere gratitude to Prof. Chris Weedon; this project would not have been possible without her brilliant expertise. I am hugely grateful to Divya Parikh for her superb and meticulous management of this project throughout. My special thanks also extend to Adeola Dewis, Nasia Sarwar, Kirsten Eve Lavine, and all the volunteers for their support. I am also grateful to Eshan Parikh for producing the films of the sixteen finalists included in this book, Catrin Edward for editing the audio scripts, Siân Trenberth for her photography, Nancy Cavill for her support, and proofreaders (Alida Payson, Sheladevi Nair, and Cathy Sampson). My gratitude to Devika Mehra, members of the EMWWAA Board, in particular Nisha Nair and Vimla Patel. My sincere thanks to Prof. Terry Threadgold for producing a comprehensive and beautifully crafted introduction; and Julie Morgan and Jane Hutt for the inspirational and eloquent foreword. I am also grateful to all our esteemed judges, and patrons, and sponsors. Finally, my sincere thanks to all the participants of this book for their generosity in sharing their personal stories and their precious time. Last but not least, our thanks to Nazma for work on the design of the cover and Richard Davies from Parthian for his meticulous professionalism and support towards marketing and publishing this book.

# Foreword

## by Julie Morgan and Jane Hutt

This book is, above all, about hope – because the life stories of the forty women featured in it will serve as inspiration for readers, whatever their background, ethnicity, age or gender. The clear message that comes through all these women's stories is to never give up, whatever struggles you face in your life's journey. As one finalist says, 'I've always seen life as an adventure, a huge learning curve'.

Some of the women whose stories are told in the book were born in far-flung places, from Mauritius to Nigeria, Hong Kong to Chile, while others were born closer to home and grew up in Butetown in Cardiff or St Pauls in Bristol. Many came to Wales knowing only their mother language. Wherever they started out, they've all made their homes in Wales and have pursued their careers here.

The book features forty finalists who have been shortlisted for awards by the Ethnic Minority Welsh Women Achievement Organisation (EMWWAA), founded by Professor Meena Upadhyaya, Honorary Distinguished Professor in the division of Cancer and Genetics at Cardiff University. The book is the result of a collaboration with her fellow Cardiff University colleague, Professor Chris Weedon.

In 2008 after attending a Welsh Woman of the Year awards ceremony, Meena was struck by the fact that there were hardly any other women from an Asian background shortlisted for an award. Afterwards, she met Julie to discuss her idea for an awards ceremony for women from Asian backgrounds – this was later broadened to all women from ethnic minority backgrounds – and both of us encouraged her to pursue this. The result was the EMWWAA awards and organisation of which we are now proud patrons.

Reading the stories of the women featured in this book, we were struck by just how many barriers some of them have had to overcome. They've faced language barriers and cultural barriers – and sometimes even barriers put up by their own community. Some viewed them as 'troublemakers' or thought they should be at home raising children. Many of these women raised families, worked and studied all at the same time – their energy and drive really shines through.

They are worthy role models for their communities and for our multi-cultural society in Wales. Their list of achievements is impressive. Some have gained multiple academic qualifications and worked in several different professions during their careers. The fields these women have entered are numerous and varied, including medicine, nursing, dentistry, academia, art, social work, politics, law and community support work. Some have forged their own paths, setting up new organisations where none existed before.

We feel that any young woman reading this book today will feel inspired by these women's fascinating stories.

As one woman said in her interview for the book, 'It doesn't matter how long it takes you to get to where you need to go – when faced with challenges, you're stronger than you think.'

**Julie Morgan**
Member of the Senedd for Cardiff North
**Jane Hutt**
Member of the Senedd for the Vale of Glamorgan

# Contents

Introduction ... 1

**Voice for the voiceless** ... **5**
Raise Your Gaze – Uzo Iwobi ... 7
Speaker for the Voiceless – Hilary Brown ... 13
Existing, Resisting and Thriving – Shavanah Taj ... 18
Crafting Independence – Martha Holman ... 24
Compassionate Courage – Maria Mesa ... 30
The Power Within – Susan Cousins ... 35
From Pain to Power – Rachel McDonald ... 41
Inspiring Change – Samsunear Ali ... 46
Joyful Giving – Poranee James ... 51
A Place of Refuge – Chetna Sinha ... 56

**Self-belief** ... **59**
Future Potentials – Meena Upadhyaya ... 61
Learning Curves – Chantal Patel ... 68
Game Changing – Gaynor Legall ... 73
Spirited Storytelling – Chandrika Joshi ... 78
Promises from the Heart – Indu Deglurkar ... 83
Healthy Living – Kamila Hawthorne ... 89
Pioneering Public Health Genomics – Layla Jader ... 94
The Way to the Future – Loren Henry ... 98
Landing on her Feet – Kiran Ratna ... 103
The Call of Music – Sarita Pawar ... 109

**Inspiring others** ... **113**
Soulful Resonance – Patti Flynn ... 115
Delivering Justice – Justna Muhith ... 120
Enacting Positive Change – Rocio Cifuentes ... 125
Life Flow – Madhvi Dalal ... 130
Positive Educational Exchange – Christina Roy ... 136
Shining a Light on Culture – Wai Fong Lee ... 141
Supportive Strength – Wanjiku Ngotho-Mbugua ... 145
Giving Life – Vernesta Cyril ... 150
Gifts of Learning – Grace Kerry ... 153
Joyful Harmony – Sunita Menon ... 158

**Forging one's path** ... **163**
The Culture of Creativity – Leanne Rahman ... 165
Vocalising Strength – Humie Webbe ... 171
Music from the Heart – Banani Sinha Ray ... 177
The Challenge of Equality – Aliya Mohammed ... 182
Youthful Engagement – Alka Ahuja ... 188
In the Spirit of Learning – Norma Glass ... 193
A World of Healthy Diversity – Diana De ... 197
Portuguese Flavours – Iolanda Banu Viegas ... 203
Strength in Diversity – Abi Lasebikan ... 207
Developing care – Versha Sood ... 211

List of judges ... 215
About Nazma Ali ... 221

# Introduction

This book has had a long and impressive gestation period involving many people and intersecting with many lives, many different countries and a huge diversity of journeys and interactions. It is the recording of that diversity as oral history, the making accessible of the narratives of women's lives, and the challenges these recorded realities offer to taken-for-granted understandings of ethnic minority women's lives in Wales which are its major achievement.

Such an achievement does not come without struggle and courage, and in this case, it always involves both the determination of those who have driven the project forward and the generosity of the tellers who have been prepared to share the complexity of often difficult stories, and amazing successes, and to show how much can be accomplished where there is a will to move beyond adversity and to contribute to and develop the country they have adopted and those in it who need support.

In 2008, Prof. Meena Upadhyaya was short-listed for the Welsh Woman of the Year Award in Science and Technology. She did not get the award, but her experience was pivotal to what happened next. She looked around the room at the awards ceremony and saw an absence; 'There were hardly any other Asian women in the room'. And from this was born the idea that there should be an award ceremony for Asian ethnic minority women in Wales. The Welsh Asian Women Achievement Awards (WAWAA) was launched in 2010, and the first award ceremony was held in 2011. Since then, thanks to Meena's own imagination, determination and dedication to the project, it has expanded to become the Ethnic Minority Welsh Women Achievement Association (EMWWAA) (emwwaa.org.uk) and to include all black and ethnic minority women and girls in Wales. The bi-annual awards have recognised many remarkable women. There have been five award ceremonies that have celebrated the achievements of eighty finalists and sixty-five winners. The forty stories represented in this book are told predominantly by winners and a few of the finalists. The first book to emerge from the project: *Her (= Challenge in Welsh) Stories* recorded the stories of the award winners in those first years (2011 and 2013). A second organisation, Ethnic Minority Women in Welsh Healthcare (EMWWH), was established later to provide educational activities and a mentoring program specifically for women in healthcare.

Prof. Chris Weedon has been the other major partner in the production of this book. Chris has been one of the judges for the WAWAA and EMWWAA Awards since 2013. Her long-standing commitment to recording and archiving the ethnic minority lives and stories that otherwise remain hidden from view in mainstream histories of Wales and its people has been a major influence and driving force in the production of this oral history. Chris herself has not been able to share in the final stages of this project. She suffered a serious brain haemorrhage in October 2020. She is now making excellent progress towards recovery but is still in the hospital. The project team have missed her input and contribution in these final months.

Chris's work with Glenn Jordan at the Butetown History and Arts Centre (BHAC 1988–2017) produced an invaluable archive of local people's memories, documents and photographs to make visible and audible the lives and stories of one of the UK's oldest multi-racial communities. The Butetown work developed some remarkably innovative methodologies and community-involvement techniques which have been transferable and used again with great success in this project to transform interviews into an engaging narrative. Family photographs, videos and audio-visual snippets of conversation available on the EMWWAA website complement the stories in this book.

This project then brings together these two strands of work on the histories and experiences of multi-ethnic Wales that shed light on the ways in which Welsh society has dealt, or failed to deal, with sexism and racism both historically and currently. What is very clear are the ways in which complex localised interactions over many years between the journeyings and experiences of ethnic minority women and the Wales they have encountered have enriched and transformed Wales itself, contributing in major ways to integration and social cohesion. The book and its narratives record an important part of the history of multi-ethnic Wales and help to chart social changes since the 1950s.

The focus is on the life stories of ethnic minority women who were born or have settled in various parts of Wales since 1948. The women who speak through the pages of this book come both from long-settled, often mixed families from various parts of Wales, including Tiger Bay (now Butetown), Ely in Cardiff (Welsh/St. Kitts in the Caribbean), Cardiff (Welsh/Barbados, Bangladesh), Swansea (Jewish origin), and women who came to Wales from settled families in other parts of the UK: Leeds (Pakistan), London (India), Edinburgh (India, Tanzania), Bristol (Welsh/Jamaican). The brackets indicate the complex origins of the settled families. They also came to Wales from all over the rest of the world: India (Delhi, Punjab, Uttar Pradesh, Mumbai, Calcutta, Tamil Nadu), Pakistan, Bangladesh, Africa (Uganda, Mauritius, Nigeria, Kenya, Zimbabwe, Mozambique), Portugal, Baghdad, Colombia, Chile, Thailand, and Hong Kong.

The diversity and the multiple layers of immigration and background involved are complex and challenging. From abroad, they come for many reasons, as asylum seekers, refugees, for arranged marriages, to study, to join husbands who are studying, as migrant workers. Nationality, family history and class, religion and educational backgrounds are remarkably different, but all seem in various ways to encounter troubling forms of racism and sexism, at school, in the workplace, in the community. This complexity totally belies the stereotypical views of immigration and its realities which remain profoundly embedded in many common understandings. As one interviewee put it, 'the media doesn't help' when ethnic minorities are regularly represented as 'snake charmers, street children, uneducated and always in poverty.'

The reality is a group of remarkable women working in every institution and area of Welsh life to effect positive change for groups of ethnic minority women and others who they see as needing the kind of support which they themselves needed as they journeyed from where they began to where they now are.

This book tells that story. The list which follows is a selection which gives some indication of what ethnic minority women's work in Wales looks like: the CEO of Race Equality First, a Consultant Child and Adolescent Psychologist, a Diversity and Inclusion Officer, nurses and lawyers, a dentist who is also a priestess and a storyteller, the Deputy CEO, Chair and Vice-Chair of Black Association of Women Step Out (Bawso), immigration lawyers, lecturers, teachers, social workers, the Councillor for Butetown, the Councillor for the UK Portuguese community, the founder of the Chinese School in Swansea, Director of Public Health, the Operational Director of Women Connect First, domestic violence and mental health advocates and advisers, the CEO of the Ethnic Minorities and Youth Support Team Wales, the Manager Citizens Advice Bureau Tiger Bay, the Society of Black Lawyers investigating racism in the profession, a cardio-thoracic surgeon, general practitioners, a pharmacist now working on period poverty, medical researchers and professors, Head of Graduate Entry in Medicine at Swansea University, Senior Compliance Advisor, Race, Religion and Belief at Cardiff University, an engineer who also dances, classical musicians and singers, dance teachers, a freelance Art consultant working with the Arts Council Wales, the Vice-President of the Royal Welsh College of Music and Drama (RWCMD), the former Chief Executive Race Council Cymru, specialist advisor on equalities to the First Minister and the Welsh Government, and the General Secretary of the Wales Trades Union Council (TUC).

Such are among the remarkable contributions that minority ethnic women have made, and are making, to Wales and its populations and some of the ways in which they have challenged the racism and the sexism, and dealt with the social, legal, medical and educational needs they have encountered. Their stories do not talk a lot about these things: their actions and their commitment do. Their life stories of struggle and achievement are a constant reminder of the huge task that remains for all of us to deal with the inequalities that harm and to fight for the equalities that matter. They speak to us through the stories in this book, offering inspiration and leadership from all the areas and corners of the social fabric and history of Wales, never losing faith in the possibility for change and always showing us the way to a better future.

**Terry Threadgold**

Voice for the voiceless

# Raise Your Gaze

## Uzo Iwobi
**PROFESSOR AND WELSH GOVERNMENT'S SPECIALIST ADVISER ON EQUALITIES**

*I'm always ready to do something new and get involved in a cause that touches my heart. I know that the Lord placed me on this earth with my energy and talents for a purpose, to be a voice for the voiceless.*

My full name is Uzoamaka, which means 'the doorway of blessing', a beautiful name that defines my identity. I was born in Mbano, South Eastern Nigeria, the fourth of five children in a very strong Catholic family. My mother had a tough upbringing, but she was very resilient, hardworking, exceptionally bright and ultimately, became the first female school headmistress in southeastern Nigeria. My father was also very bright and was a professor and the dean of the Faculty of Crop Science.

Uzo, age 2 in Nsukka, Nigeria

When I was four, both my parents won scholarships to study at an American university, and my siblings and I were left in the care of our grandmother. She was a disciplinarian and did her best to love and care for five children, but it was tough being four years old, starting school and battling missing my parents and adjusting to a grandmother in charge.

I was also very different from my siblings, who were very calm, while I was rather rambunctious, bubbly and inquisitive. I didn't fit in anywhere, and I was seriously bullied at school, especially as the other kids didn't believe my parents lived in America and called me a liar and beat me up. When my parents returned after several years, it was an experience trying to get to know them, as I was ten years old then. In secondary school, I gave my life to Christ and became a Pentecostal Christian, which was a fundamental part of discovering my purpose in life.

I went to the University of Nigeria to study for a degree in English, which I excelled at, but my father steered me in the direction of studying law as a more lucrative area of work. This was a remarkable appointment with destiny because at the start of my second year in the Law

Uzo's engagement to Andrew in Enugu State, Nigeria, 1990

department, the young and very handsome lecturer of Equity and Trusts walked into the classroom, and I turned to my friend and said, 'That is my husband.' She thought I was joking, but I'd already decided this beautiful mixed-heritage African man was the one I was going to marry. It was a match made in heaven because I am bubbly and extroverted, and Andrew is reserved, very intelligent, and a brilliant, deep, reflective thinker. He is the best thing that ever happened to me, and through him, I discovered what selfless love is. I thank God he placed me in Andrew's path because he understands my drive, determination and the absolute resolve, and he has encouraged me and shown me how to be the best that I can be.

We had a traditional, customary Nigerian wedding and registry marriage and shortly afterwards, Andrew went to the UK to start his new appointment as a law lecturer at the Swansea Institute of Higher Education. After I got my bar and solicitor's qualifications, I practised for a short period in Nigeria, while waiting for my visa to be processed, which was a battle, and we were separated for a year and a half, which was very tough. Andrew was about to resign from his job and return to Nigeria when a couple of brilliant Swansea MPs fought for me to get the visa, and I was finally able to come over.

I arrived in the UK on 7 February, my birthday. It was a shock leaving Nigeria and my family, and at 23 years old, to be so far from everything and everyone I knew. Nothing prepared me for the coldness of this country or the coldness of the hearts of some of the people I met.

The first thing I did when I arrived in Swansea was to try and get a job. I was very keen to practise law, but when I went to the job centre, I was told that law firms in Swansea would never give me a job because I was Black. I was shocked and was also asked to choose an English name and ended up using my baptismal name, Linda. I sent off many applications to numerous firms and genuinely worked hard to get in, but all to no avail. I had to go back to the job centre and was told just to put down my GCSEs and apply to places like Argos, Tesco's and Toys R Us.

I realised the battle I had in front of me. I didn't want to go on the dole, and I desperately needed a job. We had Andrew's parents living with us, and relatives back home in Nigeria waiting for us to pay for them to go to school. The first job I managed to get was as a cashier in Toys R Us. I was heavily pregnant but hid it because I didn't want to get sacked, and a month before my daughter was born, I was carrying boxes and climbing shelves. I was the most willing, hardworking and cheerful employee they had and was selected as the 'Employee of the Year'. But I also had times when some white shoppers would say they didn't want a Black person to serve them or touch their toys, which were some of the painful, racist incidents that happened to me early on.

I also secured a job packing crisps at Walkers factory

Uzo after being called to the bar as a barrister and solicitor of the Supreme Court of Nigeria, 1992

and was sent to do the worst jobs that my white colleagues refused to do. But my father had always told me that no matter where you are working or the role that you hold, do your best and be the best that you can be.

But it was a really tough culture. As a family, we faced racist bullying and abuse and moved house many times to get away from it all. Both our children, who were born in Swansea, were bullied and racially attacked on a number of occasions in their respective schools, and we had no help. Fortunately, we moved our children to other schools where racism was better addressed. At one point, you either sink or swim, and I chose to 'raise my gaze' in hope and swim. This is why I stand beside people who are disadvantaged because I know the devastating impact bullying has had on our children and ourselves.

Eventually, I got my first law lecturing job, and I taught for nine years at Swansea Law School. It was the beginning of good things, though I was still facing racism as a Black, African woman. Then I set up my first business, a training consultancy called Ofuobi, which means 'to be of one mind', and delivered a variety of training courses such as a Multicultural Awareness Course, Unconscious Bias and one on anti-racism.

When you're self-employed, sometimes you can't always be sure where the next meal is going to come from, so I thought I'd do the business on the side, and got a position as a race and diversity trainer at South Wales Police. A short while later, I applied for a secondment to a national role on the Police National Diversity Team, based at the Home Office in London. I used to come home on weekends, cook, clean, do laundry, iron and prepare food for a whole week, while Andrew kindly looked after the children while I was away. It was really hectic, and I remember the toughness of the situation and how much Andrew sacrificed for me so that I could work in London and progress my career.

I had to cut my contract short, as my children needed me, and the kids and Andrew have always been my first priority. So I came home to Swansea and became the principal equality and diversity officer for South Wales Police. We again faced a lot of bullying and racism, but we were determined to be a solution and not a problem in this society. Andrew and I taught our children to replace hatred with love and to be a light everywhere you go, though it's never easy to be a light in challenging circumstances.

Then I saw an opportunity to work for the Commission for Racial Equality as a commissioner, a role that I'd always wanted. I was talking to people in youth clubs and encouraging Black people to strive to be whatever they imagined and not to be boxed into holes. The job has opened my eyes to see that, although my kids went through enormous trauma and bullying, they are privileged to have parents who love and support them, and who educated and guided them, because many kids grow up without parental support systems.

When I completed my term in office, other Wales-based commissioners and I started an organisation called Race Council Cymru, so I was volunteering as chief executive alongside my police work and my businesses. I was initially appointed international chair for diversity for the Royal Welsh College of Music and Drama, and have just been appointed a vice president of the college. I was recruited as the first Black African to serve as a specialist adviser on equalities to the First Minister and Welsh Government. I'm so delighted for this opportunity to contribute to making this government successful.

I've also served on the board of trustees of various organisations like the British Red Cross, Bawso, United World Atlantic College, and a local environmental group called More Green Recycle Reuse. To be the ambassador for EMWWAA was a privilege, as was being named in the top 100 Black Brilliant and Welsh list by WalesOnline. I was also named in the WEN Wales 100 Welsh Women Wales list and was awarded an OBE by the Queen for my contributions to race equality and South Wales

Uzo receiving an OBE for Services to Race Equality in 2008, with husband, Andrew; daughter, Ify; and son, Chuka

communities. I've also received a First Ministers' 'Recognising Achievement Award' for promoting race equality.

My life as a lecturer, delivering training and sharing my own experience of racism across Wales, has really empowered me and opened doors for others to be mentored. And I realise why God made me such an energetic, lively person who could speak for myself with no fear. I could walk into a place with homeless people, and befriend and share with them, and I could walk into Tony Blair's cabinet and address him and his ministers, and I did in my time as a commissioner.

I'm always ready to get involved in something new and set up organisations that serve the community. I established two charities in Wales, the African Community Centre and Race Council Cymru. I also established some key groups and initiatives, such as the Black Lives Matter Wales movement and the National Black, Asian and Minority Ethnic Youth Forum for Wales. I am one of the fifty-five founders of Black History Wales 365, Zero Racism Wales Campaign, plus five multicultural hubs across Wales. I also established the leadership of the HotSeat, an educational platform offered free of charge, and a cause that touches my heart. There have also been African students who were totally displaced and living rough, and they would come and live in our house for six months, while we fed and cared for them.

I never set out to change the world, but to change the world around me, that people around me will have the sense of encouragement that I craved when I was little and to provide that sort of support. I know that the Lord placed me on this earth with my energy and talents for a purpose, to be a voice for the voiceless, and that purpose is so clear in my head that I am determined not to leave this earth without doing the best that I can to achieve it.

There is a reason why you are who you are. Don't ever let anybody try to change you because God made you unique and beautiful in your own way, and there's a path that He has for you that somebody without your qualities cannot walk, and a destiny that only you can fulfil. It's

Uzo Iwobi receiving her OBE from the Prince of Wales in 2008

okay to learn from others, but celebrate yourself and be the best version of yourself that you can possibly be, and those audacious dreams are within your reach.

# Speaker for the Voiceless

## Hilary Brown
**CEO, VIRGO CONSULTANCY SERVICES**

*I've always had a reputation as somebody who would take your side and fight your corner for you. I always try to make people feel as if they are important because everybody is.*

I was born in South Glamorgan and am from one of the older settled Black families in Tiger Bay. My great grandfathers came over from the Caribbean and Yemen in the 1890s, so we've been here for over 100 years. On my father's side, we are one of the biggest families in Tiger Bay, so we are kind of a dynasty.

My parents separated when I was very young, and I grew up in Barry with my mother and my maternal grandmother. My father, whose nickname was Flash, was a budding artist—a singer, dancer and a bit of a charmer. After the separation from my mother, he moved to London to pursue his career and wasn't in my life at all in my formative years because the divorce left my mother extremely bitter, and she refused point-blank to acknowledge him. For me, that was really quite difficult and confusing because his name was mentioned frequently in the media, as he had number one songs in the UK and was on *Top of the Pops*. It was very difficult for me to hear these amazing accolades out on the street and not be able to mention him in my house.

When I was around seven years of age, my mother remarried. My mother is a white woman and married a white man, so my siblings on my mother's side were all white, while I was the only Black child in the household and always felt very different. My needs, likes, wants, and even the music I liked were very different from my siblings, but my mother was a very bitter woman, and if I brought anything to do with my cultural heritage into the house, she'd destroy it.

I was actually quite happy in my first school. I was a very good gymnast and represented the school in all the gymnastic competitions. When my mother remarried, I had to take on the name of my stepfather, and my whole identity changed and overnight, as I was now a Catholic. I had to go to a very small Catholic school, and they tried to change the very being of who I was and everything I knew and stood for, which I found very difficult.

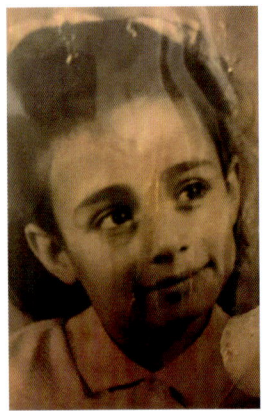
Hilary at age 8

My secondary school was also a Catholic school, and although I was happy enough and did okay, I didn't achieve near to what I could have, as I just felt totally alienated there, and the teaching didn't resonate with me. I think there were only three other Black children in the school, and I can remember the deputy headmaster saying some really awful things to me about me and my family that they could not get away with today. And nothing was done about it, which inspired me even more to be the one to challenge it.

I had a passion for speaking up for people, and I became quite boisterous and rebellious and would always stand up for people who didn't have a voice. From a very young age, I had a reputation of being a very fiery individual and somebody who would take your side and fight your corner for you, a reputation I carried all through my life. Once you've helped somebody once, people tend to signpost you as the place to go for help and refuge. I like to organise things and have them be simple and accessible. I also like people to feel comfortable within an environment, and where I saw it was not happening, I would just go in and take over.

I left school at sixteen and went to the local college. My mother had decided that she wanted me to be a secretary because that was a very good profession for a girl, but I'm really not a secretary, even though I had the skills to be a good administrator, such as the ability to type. I left the course about three-quarters of the way through because I was bored to tears.

At that time, I'd been in contact with my father's family. My mother was not happy and threw me out of the house, so I went to live with some of his family members in Tiger Bay. I also had a boyfriend and got pregnant, and had my first child when I was seventeen. We got married in London and initially lived in one room in London, at the top of a shared house. I remember walking up five flights of stairs every day with my heavily pregnant belly and thinking, gosh, there must be more to life than this.

I worked up until the time I gave birth, earning quite a bit of money, which enabled me to save and move back to Wales. I wanted my child to be born in Wales and for her to be able to be Welsh because I'm very proud of my Welsh roots. I had three children by the time I was 23. We were incredibly poor, but I settled down to being a mum and loved every minute of it and enjoyed doing things with my children because I was only a child myself. Within four or five years, I'd bought my first house and had moved a couple of times since then. I've always worked and striven to give my children a decent lifestyle.

When my last child was born, I decided to go back to college and do a sociology course and volunteered with various organisations around Barry, such as the probation service and the YMCA, as my children were very involved

Hilary's children, Mark, Spencer and Cherri, c.1990

with sports. I was also one of the founding members of the National Black Youth Forum, and my children were part of it as well, so for a lot of what I did, I included my children.

Then I volunteered with the Citizens Advice Bureau (CAB) and thoroughly enjoyed the work, representing someone in benefits or medical tribunal and taking on cases that were really devastating people's lives. I enjoyed researching, investigating and gathering evidence, but I also enjoyed empowering people to be able to do it themselves the next time or to help another person. Then I got a job with the CAB, and eventually, I became a manager of the branch in Tiger Bay (now renamed Cardiff Bay).

During that time, there was a civil war in Somalia, and lots of our clients were asylum seekers from Somalia, so I became knowledgeable and experienced in immigration law and focused a lot on this work. I quickly became the 'go to' person at the CAB for welfare benefits, employment, immigration and asylum advice, wherever there were specific race, culture or discrimination elements within a case. Quite soon, my reputation expanded beyond CAB's service, and cases were being referred to me by other organisations, including charities and individuals throughout the UK.

During my time with the CAB in the 1980s and 1990s, I became involved with the Society of Black Lawyers (SBL) and became acutely aware of allegations of racism within the legal profession. I became a colleague of and supported Rudy Narayan, who was the chair of SBL and was challenging racism within the legal profession. The difficulties he faced within the profession were hugely influential on my career path within the law.

I was offered a scholarship to qualify as a solicitor by Dr Richard Stone, one of the advisers on the Stephen Lawrence Inquiry, but I felt personally compromised by the racism within the profession, so I declined the offer. I was acutely aware of a large number of other Black people making a conscious decision not to follow a traditional route into law, and I believe that by being true to my own beliefs, I encouraged other Black people into the profession who would not ordinarily have followed this course.

During this time, I also took on a number of high-profile cases that had been referred to me, where race discrimination was considered a factor in preventing people from being treated fairly and potentially influencing the decision to deny them justice. One case challenged the police force who had failed to identify the race hate, abuse and violence that were major factors in the case.

I eventually left the CAB and worked for a number of law firms, focusing on human rights work, having identified that breaches were present in immigration and asylum decisions more than any other area of law. I chose to qualify in the various aspects of civil law that enabled me to advocate in the civil courts and tribunals where human rights was the main focus of challenge for my client group.

Hilary with councillors, Jane Hutt and Cherry Short; and MEP, Glenys Kinnock, as part of a Welsh Development Agency initiative, Cardiff Castle, 1998

I also assisted a number of law firms in setting up their immigration and asylum departments, and working in a civil department, often worked side by side with criminal departments regarding concerns of ongoing systematic failures of institutions in dealing with BAME communities. I became involved in many cases where race, culture or religion played a significant role, and I continue to receive requests nationally to assist in such cases.

During my time working at a number of law firms, I noted that nearly all of my bosses were of a certain age, class and colour and didn't have the drive and passion that I had, and I was often the only one still working at 7.30 at night. I thought, wouldn't it be great if there was a legal service driven by the needs of the clients, rather than the conventional opening office hours, so that's what I attempted to develop.

In 2008, I started my own business, a law firm called Virgo Consultancy Services Ltd, which I started from a spare bedroom in my house and now run from an office very close to home. I specialise in immigration and asylum law. It hasn't been easy, and there have been some horrendous hurdles, but there have also been some amazing achievements. It doesn't feel like work because I love what I do so much.

One of the first things I wanted to do was to become a Tier 5 licensed sponsor, so I could issue work permits to international artists, sportspeople and those within the creative industries. That drive comes from my father being a Black man within this industry, facing the most horrendous discrimination you could imagine. So I thought I would channel that inner drive to help take away some of the obstacles that international artists and sportspeople face when coming to the UK to perform and compete.

I've also probably dealt with more Caribbean and African clients than most other law firms in the UK, and have done

Hilary and her son, Mark, with the Jamaican High Commissioner, Derick Haven and wife, Thyra (*centre*), along with council officials and members of the Reggae Boys Jamaican football team at an event at the Star Leisure Centre, Splott, 1998

so for a very long time. It was clear to me that people from the Caribbean and some African countries were facing hardships because of failures, not on their part but on the part of the government. And when the Windrush scandal hit the mainstream press, I was approached by a lot of the media and was able to give a number of examples of horrible things that had happened to families, and some of them I was able to help. I've now got a reputation for being able to manoeuvre through difficult hurdles.

I'd like to develop the company to be able to do other things, particularly around discrimination, and build up a resource in terms of staff and materials. I'd like to be able to develop a pro-bono unit where if you have no money and if you fall outside of the scope of legal aid, you can still come to us, and we'll help you. That's where trainee lawyers cut their teeth and where retired lawyers can feed back their expertise. That's one of my goals, and I'm determined that I'm going to achieve it.

I always try to convince people that you are not alone. I felt very alone, and perhaps it was because of the fear and shame that I felt, I did not reach out, and I never want anybody to go through that. I've had people come to me and tell me awful stories, and I always try to make people feel as if they are important because everybody is.

# Existing, Resisting and Thriving

## Shavanah Taj
**GENERAL SECRETARY, WALES TUC**

*Don't let others draw red lines around you, particularly when you know it's not just or fair. Be brave, be bold, stand up for yourself and others. Unity and solidarity are our greatest strengths.*

I was born and raised in the great city of Cardiff. I come from a loving, working-class Pakistani family. Like many British Asians, my father arrived in the UK in the 1950s, in Sheffield, as an economic migrant from the subcontinent to counter post-war labour shortages in the mills in the north and factories in the south. Following a visit to his cousin in Bridgend, he fell in love with the South Wales Valleys, as it reminded him of being home, with the close-knit communities and luscious green valleys. He decided to lay down roots and settle in South Wales, where he would work and raise a family.

My dad worked in the Port Talbot steelworks, and my mum was the local Avon salesperson, eventually moving on to run her own business, specialising in Asian fabrics. Like many immigrants, my parents were keen to own their own home and spent years purchasing dilapidated buildings, moving us in and doing them up in between their day jobs before moving onto the next project. It took a good ten to twelve moves in my lifetime alone before they settled into their final destination in the year 2000.

As a young person coming from a South-Asian background, it was a given that you had a long list of

Shavanah's parents, Irshad Begum and Mohammed Taj, 1966

responsibilities. On weekends, while other kids would be playing outside, we would be allocated chores, including getting the food shop in, helping to tidy up, gardening duties, and caring for our younger cousins or nephews, while also helping out our elderly neighbours.

Growing up, I was one of two or three Black, Asian or ethnically diverse pupils in all three of the primary schools I attended. It was not until I went to Cathays High School that I first saw any real diversity among my peers and was no longer left with the sick feeling of 'sticking out like a sore thumb'.

As a young Asian teenager growing up in the late 1980s and early 1990s, for me, a vicious and vulgar in-your-face racism and prejudice was pretty much the norm. Our family home was often graffitied, and we even had lit fireworks thrown through our kitchen window. I still recall dodging one by seconds as it flew in past me, almost hitting my younger sister in the eye. Dog poop in supermarket carrier bags posted through the letterbox became a regular occurrence, as was racist verbal abuse, sometimes escalating to physical attacks that led to scraps on the streets. Like many families today, we did our best to report these heinous hate crimes, but nothing ever came of it. Nothing ever changed until we moved.

Such experiences meant that my personal journey into activism was almost inevitable. I recall when I was about fourteen or fifteen and on my way to school with my best mate one morning, and we were handed a 'Keep Nazis out of Cathays' leaflet. The BNP were looking to set up a youth wing, and the anti-racist league were trying to organise an alternative counter group. Despite my writing to the PO Box number listed on the leaflet, I didn't hear anything back from them, so I decided we needed to get organised and built our own anti-racist grassroots group at school.

My interest in Black history and the impact of imperialism and colonialism on African and Asian communities across the globe grew by the day. The heartache of personalised stories from elders who had lived through partition and slavery and the devastating impact and the long-standing intergenerational trauma we continue to experience today as people of colour remain a big part of why I continue the good fight for equity and social justice. The touchpoint that brought it all together was when I turned eighteen, and Stephen Lawrence was murdered. I became determined to organise and campaign against the institutional racism and discrimination that permeates and remains embedded across all structures of society.

My mum's fabric business, which she started from home, soon grew to a shop front, which my sister took over and, as a young teenager, I worked there too. When my sister was eighteen, she had an arranged marriage, which soon became extremely fraught. The pressures had a devastating impact on her mental health and wellbeing and led to a full breakdown. I supported her in getting better and took on the responsibility of helping to raise her two little boys, now young men who have become incredible adults.

Eventually, my sister divorced her husband, a highly controversial thing to do at the time, because South Asian women did not get divorced. It was a brave move, but it was the best decision she could have made and saved her life. My sister is my real-life hero and one of the most dedicated, giving people out there. She turned an awful moment in her personal life into a positive one.

We soon found out that there were several Black, Asian and ethnic minority women who needed culturally and religiously appropriate, accessible support to get out of broken and violent marriages that had collapsed. This led to us setting up the Henna Foundation, a charity that supports complex cases and the needs of women, children and families facing domestic abuse and honour-based violence. The charity is still running, and I remain an active trustee.

Having faced racism on the streets and at school, I was soon to experience it in the workplace. When I turned eighteen, I attempted to apply for a job at a retailer, following a sign in their window advertising for staff. I was turned down and told there were no vacancies, despite the fact that my white friend was encouraged to apply, though she didn't take the job. I wasn't prepared to sit down and accept the outcome, so I approached the Commission for Racial Equality and submitted a formal complaint against the business. I was soon issued a written apology with an offer of employment, which I didn't take!

Experiences of racism have continued throughout my working life, but they've become more subtle, and it's the micro-aggressions, with hidden coded language and behaviour, that remain a real issue for many working people. This is one of the reasons why I have always

The Taj siblings: Rizvanah, Shahien, Niaz, Shavanah, c.2007

supported the need for BME-led organisations fighting racism, Islamophobia and bigotry, as this is the daily lived experience for many. I feel we have a duty to remain organised and collectivised in our struggle for Wales to truly become anti-racist. My children and our future generations deserve a better, more equitable, and just Wales, in which they can live, thrive and feel accepted and whole.

My activism continued to build as I entered university to study law, followed by sociology and politics. I was the first person in my family to go to university, but thankfully, not the last. September 11, 7/7, the rise in stop and search, the deployment of the shoot to kill policy, all meant that we needed to ensure that young people and families knew what their rights were. I got involved with several grassroots organisations, including a 'stop the war' coalition and a 'stand up to racism' campaign.

After graduating, I applied for a placement with a trade

Cardiff People's Assembly anti-austerity demonstration, c.2018

union via the TUC Organising Academy. At that time, the makeup of unions was mostly white and older male, and the purpose of the academy was to attract a more diverse, intersectional base of activists from all backgrounds. My dad had been a health and safety rep in the steelworks, and as a child, I witnessed him and his comrades on strike, deep in the struggle together, and took note of how much he truly believed in unity being a strength. I was also very much aware of my ancestral history of elders who had fought against the colonialism and oppression of our people. My ingrained belief of standing up and fighting for what is right has always been there.

In 2002, following a very candid and spirited interview, the Public and Commercial Services Union (PCS) offered me a job as a union organiser in the London and the South East region, organising civil servants in Whitehall. The post was only meant to be for a year, but almost eighteen years later, I was still working as a union official at the PCS in London, having progressed through the ranks, holding several different roles across the country.

In 2011, my husband and I took the decision to move back to Wales. Living in London in our 20s was great fun, but raising children in the capital was a whole new ball game. We wanted to be back in Wales, where we had family close by and a real chance of work-life balance.

In 2018, I had the honour of being elected as the Wales TUC President, and in 2020, I was appointed as the General Secretary. The Wales TUC is the voice of Wales at work, and with forty-eight member unions, it represents around 400,000 workers. We campaign for a fair deal at work and for social justice at home and abroad.

Shavanah, with husband, Bilal and daughters, Amelia and Ariana, 2021

I am the first Muslim Asian woman in such a role, taking on the responsibility in March 2020, just as the global pandemic hit the UK. Leading the union through the social partnership structures of the Welsh Government and working with affiliated unions across all work sectors, including BME-led organisations, have been fundamental in how we ensure workers' health and safety, dignity, job security and income are protected and that all communities are supported during such extraordinarily challenging times. It's been a complete privilege to be able to be in the driving seat and work with so many incredibly dedicated and talented activists, union reps, leaders and ministers.

Being a trade unionist is no 9 to 5 job. It is built upon our collective understanding of unity and our fundamental values of internationalism and solidarity. We know that when we come together in greater numbers, we can do things like tackle bad bosses who use unfair employment practices to exploit vulnerable workers. We also educate, upskill and support workers so they can obtain good quality, sustainable jobs closer to home. We work to create a safe and supportive environment where all voices are heard at the decision-making table, and no one is left behind, while the rights of younger and older workers, Black, LGBQT+ are respected. Your 'class' or who you know shouldn't determine your access to fair work opportunities, but your ability and talent speak volumes.

As a minoritised woman, I still suffer from 'imposter syndrome,' and more often than not, I am the only person of colour in meetings and mainstream events. There are still some people who assume that my knowledge and expertise would be limited to 'equalities,' or that I'm unlikely to express a clear opinion or know how to handle difficult situations professionally and make informed decisions. Many are often left surprised!

Shavanah delivering a speech at Wales TUC, 2021

I don't believe in holding power for the sake of individual glory and having access to spaces where it's rare, almost an anomaly for a person like me, a woman and person of colour, to enter. I remain determined to always share such space and access for the greater good. I will always do my hardest to ensure others can come up behind me, but most importantly, to sit next to me. As the African–American

Shavanah, pictured with daughters, Amelia and Ariana; Meena Upadhyaya; and Maggie Simpson and Jenny Rathbone (*left of banner*), taking part in a march celebrating 100 years of votes for women, Cardiff, 2018

politician Shirley Chrisholm once said, 'If they don't give you a seat at the table, bring a folding chair'.

My dad always said to us, 'Nobody is better than you, and regardless of what people may say to you, always stand up for yourself, even if it feels like you're not supposed to, or you might be deemed a troublemaker. It's still important that you stand up for yourself.'

# Crafting Independence

## Martha Holman
**FOUNDER, LOVE ZIMBABWE CHARITY**

*I'm passionate about my culture and wanted to do something back home to empower people, help them earn sustainable incomes, and do something to help women have the independence that I'd never had.*

I was born in Harare, Zimbabwe, and we lived in a Black township. We were four in my family, two sisters and two brothers. My parents split when I was nine years old, and I decided to live in the village with my grandparents. My grandmother was a very strict Christian Methodist, and it was a really harsh lifestyle. I had to do all the chores for the house, fetching firewood and milking the cows in the morning before I went to school. I was like a little slave, but my grandmother made me a very focused, honest and principled person. So, it was a tough life, but it was good for me because it built the person I became.

At primary school, I was one of the bright children in the class. I knew my grandparents were struggling, so maybe that's where my passion for selling started. My grandfather was into growing fruits, and in the morning, I would carry a huge bag of mangoes to school and sell them at break time to help my grandparents with my school fees. So, I was known as a seller in the primary school.

My father promised that whatever happened, I was going to get the best education, and he stuck to his word. I wanted to go to boarding school at

Martha (*left*) with friends at Sandringham High School, 1987

the age of twelve, and my father agreed. This was the start of me living on my own. I went to Sandringham High School, one of the very expensive schools in Zimbabwe, and to pay the fees, my father had to sell his bed. There was a point where he couldn't pay for my school fees, but he would do anything for me to stay in that school.

When I was waiting for my school results, I fell pregnant. So, I became a teenage mother, and my father was incredibly angry with me and threw me out of the house. I went to live with my mother, and I met someone who said he would marry me with the child, but he didn't want me to work. We married, but I thought, I did so well in school, I've got to do something and be independent.

In 1990, I applied to become a teacher. I was very excited to get an interview at Belvedere's Technical College, which used to be a white-only school before the country's independence. That's one thing Mugabe did for us, that Black people could go to these colleges that used to be only for white people.

When I went for my interview, I was pregnant with my second son. When they asked me if I was pregnant, I said no, as I was wearing a big African dress. I got a place, and they never found out. Luckily, my baby was born on a Friday, so I had Saturday and Sunday before I went back to college. I had a room at the college and had a girl helping me with the child. Sometimes I would bring my son and helper with me to college, and at lunchtime or even in the middle of lessons, I would go and feed him. I never took time off, and thankfully, there were no issues.

Over the years, my husband and I had lots of problems and divorced after my third child, a daughter, died of meningitis. I managed to get a house from the Ministry of Education, and that's when my life became more independent, realising I was on my own with my two boys, aged eight and six.

Three years later, I got in trouble, with Mugabe's government accusing me of teaching politics. I was beaten up and taken to the police station, put in a cell and interrogated. I had a friend from Carmarthen I'd met when she had visited Zimbabwe, and when she saw the problems that I was having and that my life was in danger, we talked about the possibility of me coming to the UK.

As I had been teaching for quite a long time, I applied for vacation leave and was given three months' advance pay, which I left with my father to look after my children. I arrived in the UK on the 27th of January. It was freezing cold and very windy. My friend, Samara, lived in a barn with a chimney, and it caught fire the very day that I arrived. We lost everything, apart from our passports and a basket full of arts and crafts that I had brought with me. We then had to live in a two-berth static caravan with Samara's eight-year-old daughter for the next five months. During this period, a lot of my family members died due to HIV/AIDS, including my third sibling, and I found myself helpless being so far away. In search of peace and solace, I spent lots of time on my own in the Preseli Mountains.

I had come to Wales on a six-month holiday visa, and when it came to an end, although I missed my children, I made the difficult decision to stay in the UK because of the rising crisis in Zimbabwe. I could have claimed refugee

Martha and her friend, Samara, climbing Pen-y-Fan Mountain, in support of people from Domboshawa, Zimbabwe, 2019

status, as I had every proof that I was blacklisted by Mugabe's government. But I was adamant that I wanted to go back home at some stage, and I worried that if I became a refugee and something happened to one of my sons, I might not be able to get back. At one point, I travelled and met my children and my mother in Zambia.

I've always worked day and night for my father and for my sons. I know sometimes it affects me that I didn't bring my children, but I think they are happy where they are now, especially my first son, who manages a community centre through my charity, Love Zimbabwe. The whole community knows him, and he loves working with the land, so I feel like this is where he belongs. I'm hoping I can bring my second son over because he wants to do more education and get a professional job.

When I was teaching in Zimbabwe, I had started working with a group of women who'd been left on their own with their children. I taught them how to tie-dye cloth, and we made T-shirts and batik cloth that I used to take around to different African countries to sell, like South Africa, Malawi and Tanzania, and I would bring back food supplies for these women.

The project continued when I came over to the UK. I went to London and moved in with Samara's friend, who helped me sell my batiks to an African shop in Brixton. I was offered a place to study at a local college, so I was able to extend my visa as a student. Then I got a job as an au pair and lived with a family for two years, looking after the woman's three children, two of whom were boys similar in age to mine.

Then I started doing markets at weekends, selling handmade African arts and crafts. So I was looking after the children during the week, and at weekends when I was free, I used to do various markets, like Greenwich, Merton Abbey Mills, Peckham and Camden. Over time, I became unwell and stopped being able to look after the children. The manager of Merton Abbey Mills became a friend, and he offered me a room in his house and money to develop my business.

I never thought I would marry again after what I'd experienced in Zimbabwe. But I met my husband, David, at Merton Abbey Mills market. We both love music and became friends and got close. We went to Zimbabwe together in April 2004. My father's house had been destroyed under Mugabe's 'Operation Restore Order', and everything was upside down, and my children had nowhere to sleep. I took Dave to the villages which had no electricity, toilets or anything. He had never seen poverty in that context, and that was the beginning of the Love Zimbabwe charity. We got married in 2007 at Lake Chivero in Zimbabwe, a traditional marriage with a paid *lobola*, and I hope, touch wood, he'll never control me because he paid fourteen cows for me! We have another child, and Dave changed my life completely, making me believe in myself and always encouraging me for the best.

When my daughter died of meningitis in 1998, I decided I wanted to help other women because, in African communities, some women are like slaves to their husbands. So I decided the rest of my life I wanted to support women, especially those with disabled children because my doctor told me my daughter would have been mentally disabled. When I came to the UK, I knew that I wanted to do something back home to empower people and help them earn sustainable incomes and for women to have the independence that I'd never had.

The situation in Zimbabwe has not improved, and there is little tourism. People make beautiful arts and crafts, but markets were destroyed by the government, and craftspeople have nowhere to sell their products. That's why I started a charity and community interest company, which raises awareness about the situation back home and sells arts and crafts products. It's called Love Zimbabwe because it's built on the love of the people of Zimbabwe. We import arts and crafts to the UK and sell them, and our profit goes back into community projects. This, alongside the funding we've received from the Welsh Government and various other funders, has enabled us to build a community centre in Chinamhora, Zimbabwe, in an eco-friendly African style, where we teach the community how to grow food organically.

We have recently built a library with facilities for disabled people and sent a seventeen-seater bus, which was full of books because these children have got no access to education at all. We also look after disabled children because that's my passion, supporting them using the community centre facilities and training the mothers on how to look after the children.

I've also been working with schools as a Fairtrade producer and teaching young people how to make Zimbabwean batiks. It's about empowering people in the UK, as well as raising awareness so they can see how lucky

Martha and Love Zimbabwe trustee, Angeline Tshiyane, discussing the work of the charity with Welsh First Minister, Carwyn Jones, Cardiff, 2018

Martha giving a presentation on Fairtrade products at Plasmawr School in Cardiff, 2018

they are, whereas, in Africa, they've got no opportunities.

Because I'm so passionate about my culture, I've also introduced a cultural exchange project, where I take university students to Chinamhora village. When I was growing up, an equal relationship between a white and a Black person didn't exist, so when I bring people to the village, I'm trying to create the understanding that we are equal, regardless of colour. We do outreach work and talk to people, and when we come back to the UK, we raise money for projects, like helping people who have nothing to live on to renovate their houses.

Tables have turned upside down, and now, the whole village relies on me, yet when I was growing up, I was like the black sheep of the family, but I never lost hope. I've always believed in the power of education, and I even did my Master's degree when I was forty-something and also got my

Martha cheering with pupils of Nyakudya Primary school, Zimbabwe, after giving a talk about the importance of education, 2017

PGCE. Now I teach Independent Living Skills to disabled adults in Wales. I managed to send my two brothers to university and am in the process of building a school for the disabled in Chinamhora. It's a way of giving back to my father what he gave me, and if he were alive, my father would have been happy that I managed to accomplish what I wanted in life.

The advice I give to girls in the village is to stay focused. Life is not easy but don't lose hope in whatever you do. Life is a rollercoaster, but never give up. Always be determined. Whatever you have in life, whatever you plan to do, you will succeed.

# Compassionate Courage

## Maria Mesa
**OPERATIONAL DIRECTOR, WOMEN CONNECT FIRST**

*I feel the pain of humanity in my heart. But I always find myself working with amazing people who have so much character and courage. There's always a light, even if you can't see it at the time, and there is always a reason for things happening.*

Maria, First Holy Communion, aged 7

I was born in Medellín, a big city in Colombia, and I come from a very large, loving family. My grandfather was an amazing man and my hero. He was born into a very poor family, the eldest of seven children. When he was sixteen, he left his small village deep in the Andean hills, and over time, he managed to qualify as an accountant and eventually became the President of Colombia's accountant. He married my grandmother and supported her family too, and it was like a beautiful love story their whole lives. He never judged other people and I always feel that he's next to me, protecting me.

I'm the second of four girls. My mum and dad didn't have any sons, but they were really happy with us. My mum was eighteen when they got married. She was a woman ahead of the times and always worked, either with my father, who was a computer engineer, or with my granddad in the accountancy business.

My dad is an amazing, beautiful man and has always been a feminist and supported us. And even though we lived in this very macho society in Colombia, my dad always cooked, washed the dishes, ironed and cleaned the house. We also had chores, but if we were studying, he'd say, don't worry, you just study and give me your work. So I always had that kind of role model, which was amazing.

I was really lucky to be growing up in a middle-class family, where the values of education were important, and they had the resources to educate me. It was tough, but I was able to go to very good private schools. My parents had very high expectations of us, and we were expected to go to university and be professionals. My sisters and I are privileged women to have had that kind of education and background.

Maria with her parents, sister and brother-in-law, celebrating her mum's 80th birthday in Penarth, 2012

I was a very good student, but my first memory of the convent school is of the Spanish nuns telling us in history class that the Spanish people came to South America to civilise us. When I was fourteen, I started to read lots of books on colonialism, and it was like a shock to my system to find out how the colonial powers and Catholic Church were extremely cruel and horrible. I had to write an essay about neo-colonialism, and at the end of my essay, I said that when the Spanish came to the Americas, they enslaved and killed us and gave us diseases and raped us, so who are the savages? My parents were called to the school and I was asked to apologise, and I didn't, so the school expelled me.

My parents were very angry with me for being a disappointment because I was rebelling against the educators. My uncle helped me find another school, which was run by crazy, revolutionary nuns. It was really great, and my revolutionary spirit really developed. I became a member of left-wing organisations and women's movements, and it was a very exciting time for me. I decided to give up religion as well and became an atheist, and though my family was very traumatised, it was my choice.

When I was eighteen, I went to the National University of Colombia and studied sociology. Che Guevara came to my university when I was there. I became part of different groups and was out all the time marching and protesting for a better country. I supported trade union movements and went to all the shanty towns to work with communities, demanding clean water and services. Then lots of people started getting killed in the process of the revolution. When I was 20, three of my best friends disappeared in one of the marches. I went looking for them in the police stations and couldn't find them. Three months later we found my friends' bodies, mutilated, which was quite traumatic. I became known to the police and they started a 'dirty war' against me with my family, saying they wouldn't be responsible for my security if I disappeared, so I should leave the country. My family were very worried about me. For six months, I refused to leave since I felt this was my country and my future. One night we discovered they were coming to get me, so I had to leave quickly.

My sister was living in Wales at the time, so I came here.

It was so traumatic because I didn't speak any English at all and I found it really tough to adapt. It took me a long time because I didn't want to be here, and I found people were not welcoming, and I felt like I didn't belong. It was really very difficult for me because I always felt like my life had been cut off and taken away from me, and it just felt so unjust. It's the story of many people in this world who are still going through similar things, and my story is not as bad as many others. So I always have so much empathy for people who come here, and I feel the pain of humanity in me and in my heart.

I got a job in Barnardo's in the Multicultural Women's Cultural Centre, where I worked for about five years. This was the first BME women's centre in Wales and I had the most amazing time there. Through Barnardo's, I was lucky to get a secondment to go to university and I studied social work. So I became a qualified social worker and was really happy.

Then I worked for Voluntary Action Cardiff for about eight years. That was a really good experience, working with and empowering various Black and ethnic community groups, so it was really lovely and I really liked the job. I was working with amazing people who have so much character and courage. I always think that I meet the right people in my life, and they became my family and helped me through the tough times in my life.

I'm also a founding member of Bawso (Black Association of Women Step Out), which took us five years to establish. Bawso opened in July 1995 and is now one of the most successful organisations in Wales and provides so many services for BME people. For me, they are a kind of rock for the community. I was also a founding member of the Black Voluntary Sector Network Wales and a director for about six years, as well as a trustee of a refugee council, so I was really active in lots of different groups. I don't know where I had the energy because I was getting divorced at the time and had a young son. But even in the middle of all this, I think my 30s and 40s were the most productive and exciting years of my life.

Maria (*middle*), around age 35, with her sisters, Anna Maria and Claudia, in the family home on a visit back to Colombia

For me, the frontline services is where I thrive. I'm the kind of person who has lots of ideas, and I like starting things and handing them to people to move on and take in their own direction. I don't like to stay too long in places and I like change and innovation. My management style is to let the staff figure out what to do and to come back to me if something doesn't work. But most of the time things work because people are creative and committed to making them work and do everything possible.

Now I'm at Women Connect First, as director. I've got a

group of women who are absolutely amazing and very hard workers. We went through a funding crisis where we had to decrease our hours and our salaries, and we all stayed and worked harder than ever trying to save the organisation. We're still looking after 300 women every week who come through our doors, and we've managed to do it with the help of volunteers making the machinery of it work.

We have a lot of respect for each other. We are all in the same boat, from ethnic minority communities, and some of the women in my office are themselves facing issues of discrimination or domestic violence and they're still giving. The resilience of these women is so remarkable, and we all support each other as a family.

Maria with Women Connect First staff, 2018

My inspiration is every single woman who comes through the door of Women Connect First. There are women who are in a huge crisis, with more painful stories than mine. We give them a sense of belonging, and a touch of humanity and love, to say, you are worth it, your life is valid.

I'm 64 now and I want to retire soon, but I think there's so much to be done. I'm looking at supporting women in the community of all ages to become leaders and be confident to take over. I hope we are able to work together and see a better world for our future generations.

I'm also proud of my son who's become a beautiful human being. He's an environmental and human rights lawyer and very rich in love and generosity. So for me, that's one of my biggest achievements, that I helped this human being become a loving, compassionate, generous person, and I hope that he carries the legacy of love, compassion and generosity with him to the world.

I think in the short term, I just want to be happy. I'm a happy person, and I accept my past and my present. My advice is to keep the fire going. Never give up and keep your spirits growing, always. There's always a light, even if you can't see it at the time, and there's always a reason for things happening. And sometimes it takes a long time, like it took me twenty years to realise I'm here in the UK for a reason, and you realise you become grateful for all the good things that you have in your life, and the things that are not so good, try to transform them.

It's acknowledging as well that we're lucky to have the strength of character or personality to deal with life

Maria with her partner, Cliff and her son, Gareth Camilo, at home in Canton, 2020

challenges. There are some people who need to be held and taken through dark times and through tunnels and to show them the light. For me, it's been acknowledging that this is important, and I hope that one day someone will also hold my hand and take me through.

# The Power Within

## Susan Cousins
**SENIOR COMPLIANCE ADVISER, RACE–RELIGION AND BELIEF, CARDIFF UNIVERSITY**

*My focus has always been on the people who get left behind and don't get to thrive in our society. There are people suffering in this society and culture, mostly around loneliness, isolation and a constant feeling of not fitting in. So I'm never going to live a life that's not about supporting others.*

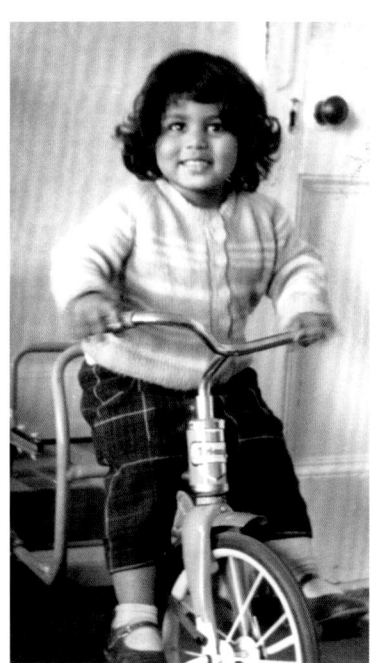

Susan with her new tricycle, age 2

I was born in India and found on a pavement in the streets of Mumbai. I was picked up by the police and taken to an orphanage in Mumbai, where I stayed for under a year. I was adopted by a couple, an English woman and an Irish man, who were working in India at the time. They'd already adopted two children—one from a Bangladeshi background and another mixed-race Bangladeshi.

It took a long time before my parents could adopt me, as I was severely ill and suffering from malnutrition from being so poorly fed in the orphanage. I don't know exactly when we came to the UK, but I was in the tropical medicine hospital in London for a lot of treatment. Then, with my father being Irish, we went to live in Ireland for a while. Afterwards, my parents adopted five more children from varying backgrounds, all children of colour, and we moved to England.

My parents were wonderful people in some respects, but however much I love my mother and father and really appreciate what they did, I don't think children should be transported over to different countries to fulfil the needs of people who can't have children. I lost a lot of things when I was adopted—my language, my family and my heritage. I gained my life and an amazing family, and for that I'm forever grateful, but I think what's really needed is for the political circumstances in India to change, so children don't end up on pavements and in orphanages. The life of a transnationally adopted person is often quite fragile, and where attachment to anything solid feels almost impossible at times.

Susan (*second from the left in front*) pictured with her mother, siblings and friends on a visit to a nearby village in Bangladesh, 1968

I was brought up in a small town, and because it was predominantly white, and I think only one other Asian person living there, it was an isolating experience. We were such an unusual family, with two white parents and seven adopted children from different countries who all looked different from each other. We were thrown into the limelight with interest from magazines, radio and television, and we were filmed for *Panorama*. So we were raised in a town where it was impossible to feel anything other than incredibly visible. I would describe this both as feeling a sense of belonging and of not belonging. I was always aware of the differences and felt thrown against this white landscape, maybe more so because I was the darkest child.

From a young age, I wanted to be a doctor and, when I grew up, to return to India to work. I can't remember a time that I didn't want to be helping and supporting other people. I remember going to children's homes with my parents, who were in the process of adopting other children, and I was surrounded by the idea that people were not born into the world equal and that there was a lot of cruelty and tragedy in the world.

I was continuously bullied at school, especially the Catholic grammar school I went to when I was eleven. I was the only brown girl in a school of 1,500 girls, so I didn't stand a chance. I was harassed and spat on in the playground, so it was impossible for me to go to school. I spent most of my time playing truant and avoiding school at any cost. I think there was one year when I barely went to school at all. I just walked around town, hid in car parks and department stores—I don't know why nobody noticed, but I became quite resilient and determined not to put up with the bullies. Later, after I left that particular school, I became very good at netball and art, so I found a way to survive. I was also brought up in a house full of books, so

Susan, finding the confidence to take a holiday in Italy, 1998

books were my go-to safe place. But I don't think any of my siblings made close friends at school either, and it was a really difficult time for us all.

Even without going to school much, I managed to pass my exams and went to university in London. It was another impossible situation, as I was the only brown student in my college and halls of residence and was bullied again. I made one friend, who I'm still friends with and absolutely adore, and he helped me out enormously. But it was just too difficult in those days when there was no awareness of the impact of racism on our lived experience. I tried to stay at university, but it was impossible, so I gave up.

I went on to have two children and lived in Bradford for a while, but my husband and I ended up in Cardiff because he was doing a Master's in English at Cardiff University. It felt like a nice city, but we were living in significant poverty, so it was a very tough period of my life.

I've always found solace in being creative, mostly painting, while I also did lots of voluntary work. I helped at one of the Saturday schools for children of colour and worked for what was called, at that time, the Community Relations Council. I did some training for South West Yorkshire Police in Leeds when I was in my early 20s, and I used to volunteer looking after older people. I later worked for the unemployment centre in Cardiff a couple of days a week. I was trying to forge a career for myself because I had nothing; really, apart from my two wonderful children and my family, I didn't have a career.

I eventually trained to be a counsellor and did the first year of my CSCT diploma in Bristol and the second year in Cardiff at Whitchurch Hospital. I decided that I wouldn't write a single essay without it being about people of colour. The tutors would tell me I'd written brilliant essays about BAME issues but that they didn't meet the criteria. But I wasn't interested in meeting the criteria, but about the psychology and wellbeing of people of colour. However, I scraped through the course enough to get the diploma and eventually went on to become a senior accredited counsellor and supervisor with the British Association for Counselling and Psychotherapy.

I was the first brown counsellor in the whole of South Avon to be employed by the council, and that was a fantastic experience. I worked for nine NHS general practices in the centre of Bristol, near St Pauls. I only saw Black and brown clients, and it was a huge privilege to hear their individual stories and to play a part in their process of healing.

Since 2008, I've been working at Cardiff University, both as a counsellor and later in the field of race, religion, and belief. The university has been an amazing place for me to work. It's a predominantly white organisation, and in that sense, it has its challenges, but it's such an interesting and challenging environment, and I've met some amazing people. The role involves providing specialist advice and guidance to the university through many channels. For example, I established the Race Equality Supervisory Panel, which provides an innovative approach to dealing with incidents where race shapes the issue. I also deliver recommendations across the university using my judgement and creative ability to deliver a fresh approach to engagement with the race-equality agenda.

In 2019, I published a book called *Overcoming Everyday Racism, Building Resilience and Wellbeing in the Face of Discrimination and Microaggression*. The book treads the path between the relational, on the one hand, and the political, on the other. There was nothing for me to turn to when I was growing up, so this book is for BAME people to have something to help them. It has tools for finding your own way and managing the impact of racism, so there are lots of reflections and exercises to help support people and find solutions that are authentic to their individual experiences.

I hope the book will provide solace, comfort, and reflection for people of colour because the experience of racism has a huge impact on our wellbeing and mental health. I also hope it provides a space to hold a conversation with oneself about race and encourages an internal dialogue that will support individuals in building and leading a good enough life.

Susan at the launch of her book, *Overcoming Everyday Racism*, the event hosted by Cardiff University, 2019

Engaging with people and having deep meaningful encounters is hugely important. Hence, I want people to meaningfully engage with my book to get support in the same way they'd engage with a human being. Life is all about connectedness and relationships, and I've come across some remarkable white people in my life who have been amazing allies and some people of colour who've also been wonderfully supportive.

But we need to look at our own lived experiences as people of colour, the impact of racism on our lives, and then produce our own material about how it impacts on us emotionally, rather than have it written about by people who don't have that lived experience. That said, I've also heard from a lot of white people who love the book because they are learning about the experiences of people of colour having been written in an accessible way and are thinking about things completely differently as a result. So, although it's a book primarily for people of colour, it's also a book for everybody.

I love Wales, and it has treated me extremely well during the 25 years I've lived in Cardiff, including the time I was shortlisted for an EMWWAA award. On the other hand, my children and granddaughter live in England, so I hope to move to be nearer to them when I am able to. I'm also extremely proud of my Indian heritage and having come from Mumbai. My mother and father told me I came from Dharavi, a Mumbai shanty town made famous by the hit film, *Slumdog Millionaire*. So those are my roots, and I feel that India rescued me and gave me life. I want to go back to the orphanage where I came from and be more involved with it. To return to India would be a hugely traumatic experience, which I couldn't have done at a young age. I can do it now because I feel grounded and rooted in who I am.

My advice to people is to take small steps in your everyday life. Make sure you get up and get dressed every morning, and go about your everyday life with mindfulness, eat well, walk, run or swim. Look after yourself as well as you are able to, so you build enough resilience to welcome another day. Try to keep a diary, make friends, and build relationships where you can. People should be proud of keeping their everyday lives going, and to me, it's a fundamental part of how you can build wellbeing into everyday life. I take every day as it comes and mostly want to live a quiet life.

Finding meaning in your past and present life, and knowing your direction of travel and where you are headed provides us all with a source of strength that helps to keep us on track. I feel like a work in progress and not the finished article.

# From Pain to Power

## Rachel McDonald
**INDEPENDENT DOMESTIC VIOLENT ABUSE ADVOCATE**

*I think when you've been in a position where life is hard and challenging, it can put you down. It's all about that climb back up, which can be equally hard because it can be two steps forward, one step back. But I would say to people to do the best that you can and to be gentle with yourself, which I think is really important and gets lost. We're too busy trying to please others and we should be pleasing ourselves.*

I was born in Bristol. My mother is white Welsh from the Rhondda Valleys and my father is Jamaican, and came over as a child in the late 1950s, as part of the Windrush generation. I have two younger sisters and a brother. For my first few years, we lived in an area called St Pauls, which had a multicultural atmosphere, and you didn't feel as though you were the only mixed-race person, as there were Sikhs, Hindus, Chinese, Asian and Black people. I also used to love the St Pauls Festival.

When I was five or six, we moved to a different area called Easton. It was a trying time, as my parents were having difficulties and my father left, and things changed massively. My mother worked as a cleaner in the early days, bringing up four kids on her own. She worked really hard, and that internal strength and work ethic has influenced me to persevere through certain challenges that are presented to me.

At home, I had a lot of responsibility of helping to look after my siblings when my mum was working, so I liked the school because I had a bit of freedom and could be my own age. My senior school was St Mary Redcliffe and Temple School, one of the best state schools in Bristol. My mum fought tooth and nail to get me in since we were outside of its catchment area. I liked that school and felt quite a sense of gratitude to them because they were very helpful to my mother, who was struggling financially, so I didn't miss out on school trips to places like France and Holland.

Rachel age 12, holding her brother Eugene, standing next to sisters, Fay and Naomi (*in front*), at their home in Bristol, 1988

I loved netball and swimming and was a

prefect. But when I was fifteen, I had a boyfriend and got pregnant, so what was tough before became even tougher. I was a big girl and hid my pregnancy and didn't tell anyone. It only became known when I passed out in front of my mother when I was seven months' pregnant. It was the summer holidays and I got a cleaning job with my mother at my old primary school. Within eight weeks, my mother had everything ready for my son, and with my cleaning money, we bought the best pram that money could buy.

I had my son, Rhys, in September 1991 and was back in school in January. I did okay in my GCSEs and gained enough to go to Brunel College in Bristol. I did a BTEC in National Health and Social Care. It was very hard, but social services were really good at providing childcare. After that, in early 1995, I ended up coming to Wales to live because I wanted to spend the time with my grandparents, who I loved to bits and usually only saw during holidays. They were very supportive and helped out with looking after Rhys.

Then I moved to a council estate, and it was like a concrete jungle. There were very few people of colour, and there was a lot of racial abuse. It was a very trying time in my life, and though I was resilient to a point, I felt like I was a fish out of water and that I didn't belong there. I soon moved to Tonyrefail, became pregnant again and was once again on my own, with no support. I had my second child, my daughter Lowri, when Rhys was eight.

For me Tonyrefail was a difficult place to live. It was always a challenge just to have normal conversations about the weather, which I think is a mindset in smaller communities, living in each other's pockets. I like the community element, and when someone needs support, then that generosity and spirit are there, but not if you're someone different outside the norm and don't fit in. They made me feel like I wasn't Welsh enough. But it wasn't all bad. I've got good, firm friendships with one or two people that are still there, but they're of a mindset that is exceptionally open.

I had always wanted to be a nurse or a social worker because I wanted to help others. Once I had my own child, I knew I could look after someone else's if they had the need. I think when you've been in a position where life is hard and challenging, it can put you down. It's all about that climb back up, and that can be equally hard because it can be two steps forward, one step back, so you've got to make the best of it. It was just having the time and space to allow myself to develop outside of my role as a mum. I didn't become a nurse or a social worker in the end, but those aren't regrets because what I do now I absolutely love.

In 1995, I got a job as a home care assistant for a local authority and, then, as an admin assistant for a local education authority. Then, in 2006, I worked as a social worker assistant for Newport City Council, which was very challenging and intense but rewarding. I was trying to engage with young parents like myself, helping them to be a mum but also showing them that there can be more to an individual than just being a teenage mum.

In 2008, I had another child, my daughter, Crisian. The following year, I met my partner, who began living with us. For the first couple of years, our relationship was fantastic, and the family got on great. Then in 2010, my son Rhys got

into the University of Lancaster, which was a very big deal. He graduated with a 2.1 in Sports Development, and I was really chuffed for him. But when he was away at university, I started experiencing physical violence at home. This went on for another four or five years. I hid most of it, and I think in that time, I only called the police once. I think that I was on autopilot during that period of my life because I was quite unwell and probably suffering from undiagnosed clinical depression. In the meantime, to escape the house a bit, I picked up my education. In 2014, I became qualified as a Level 4 practitioner in therapeutic counselling and, three years later, attained my PGCE.

In 2014, I was referred to Bawso, who were specialists in domestic abuse for Black and minority ethnic people. I did their recovery toolkit programme, a twelve-week CBT-focused psychological approach to counselling, which involved women sharing their stories and journeys and which was very insightful. What I really liked about the course was that you realise that you're not alone and I felt as though I belonged there, because I felt excluded living in the Valleys. I met some wonderful women and facilitators of the toolkit programme, a couple of whom are still my friends now. So the course was part of my healing journey, and probably the reason I stayed to volunteer was to continue having that sense of belonging.

I became involved in fundraising activities for Bawso and, then, I was asked to be a board member, and in 2017, to be vice-chair. Having recently been through

One of Rachel's fundraising activities for Bawso, running a Cardiff Half Marathon, 2018

Rachel at work as an IDVA at Safer Merthyr Tydfil, Domestic Abuse Resource Team

one of the most horrific experiences of my life, Bawso changed my world. There was no judgement there. You were encouraged to do the best that you could, and it built up my confidence and self-esteem. When you're in an abusive relationship, you're quiet because when you speak up you know what's going to come. So what Bawso did was to give me back my voice.

More recently, I was involved with RISE, a domestic abuse service in Cardiff and, in a year-long post, gained professional practice supporting women and girls who were experiencing domestic abuse. For the past couple of years, I've been a special domestic court independent domestic violent abuse advocate (IDVA) in Merthyr, supporting women who are going through domestic abuse or post-separation and are pursuing a complaint through the criminal justice system.

I also support women who are at high risk of serious harm, so that each client receives the appropriate service for their needs while also ensuring safety for them and their children. I help provide advocacy, as well as emotional, practical support, and information for clients regarding legal options, housing, health and finance and recovery programmes.

I'm ambitious and would like to be a manager, but ultimately, I'm a front-line worker and am impassioned by this work because I've been there, and knowledge is power. I wasn't aware of the services that were available to enable me to seek help until I went through it myself.

I'm still a fish out of water, but I don't feel so singled out or isolated because I know where I am. I think that comes with confidence, and I feel more empowered and self-assured. I'm human, I'm fallible, so I have good and bad days, but I think I've learnt not to be so hard on myself because I am my biggest critic.

My three magnificent children have been a great support to me and have motivated me to be a better mum and a better person. They've picked me up when I've been down, wiped my tears and held me and loved me when I didn't love myself. I've supported them too, emotionally and practically to the best of my ability, as a single mum. Rhys is now employed as a civil servant and is a father himself. Lowri is in her third year at Swansea University, and Crisian is in year 8 at Hawthorn High. I am eternally grateful to them—they have saved me too.

When you have regrets, you have guilt, and it's not that I don't want to feel guilt, but I don't want to be indebted to it all the time. I want to move on and to grow from it, and make more positive changes to my life. I would say to people to do the best that you can and to be gentle with yourself, which I think is really important and gets lost. We're too busy trying to please others and we should be pleasing ourselves.

Rachel receiving an EMWWAA award from the First Minister Mark Drakeford in 2019.

Family photo featuring (*left to right*) daughter, Lowri; Rachel, son, Rhys; granddaughter, Ariya; and daughter, Crisian, 2019

# Inspiring Change

## Samsunear Ali
**DEPUTY CEO, BAWSO**

*I don't believe anybody else can make you happy. You have to make yourself happy and to be able to achieve. I think it's about challenging yourself, following your dream, and as long as you're not doing anything bad, don't let other people put boundaries within your life.*

I was born in Cardiff, the oldest of six siblings. Growing up was interesting, as it was a bit of a clash between East and West. When we were younger, we frequently travelled back home to Bangladesh. Although we were born here, my dad truly believed in not forgetting our heritage. So for me, I still feel that I have that connection of belonging to a larger family and wider network where everybody knows you, and you know where you stand within the family setting. I think this is quite important for your own identity.

We would stay in Bangladesh for a year or two at a time, and I would go to school there and have tutors in Bengali and Arabic. My dad made sure we didn't forget the culture, but at the same time, I missed out on a big chunk of my British education. As a result, my English became terrible, so I really found it difficult to communicate in school when we came back. The frequent travelling happened for the first ten or eleven years of my life during primary school, but once I was in high school, my dad felt he couldn't disrupt our education, so we stayed in the UK for the full stretch of secondary school education.

I went to Cathays High School, which was predominately

Samsunear, second from the left, in a family photo at Eid, 1989

mainstream in its makeup at the time, with only a few ethnic minority families, my cousin's and my family being the only Bangladeshis. I remember the children couldn't pronounce my name, and they would sometimes make fun of me and call me 'Satsuma.' At the time, I had a bit of a Bangladeshi accent, so I was embarrassed to put my hand up and interact in class, just in case somebody made fun of my accent. The teachers didn't do much, as they probably thought it was just children making a joke, so I just spent the first few years there getting on with my work and not making many friends. That was my first experience of racism, of not feeling a part of the UK society because I was different, had an accent and felt that I couldn't aspire.

My dad had wanted me to do medicine, but I was made to feel that I was not capable. I then convinced myself that this was my dad's dream, not mine. So instead, my parents decided to marry me off and, at the age of eighteen, I was taken to Bangladesh to get married. They gave me a choice of who I wanted to marry, and I chose my first cousin. I could see that he was a humanitarian and very aspirational in how he spoke about life, so I thought maybe it wouldn't be so bad after all and I could get on with this person.

After we got married, we lived in Bangladesh for two years until I was expecting my first child. I came back to the UK because I was afraid of having my child back home, as I didn't trust their medical system, and I thought I'd have proper support here in Cardiff. My husband soon followed me, leaving his career as a solicitor in Bangladesh. It was a big step for him, as he was doing so well there, but he came along to where I wanted to be. Once in the UK, he went to university and requalified as a solicitor, as his Bangladeshi qualification was not recognised here. Even then, he never quite managed to secure a career in this profession, so he became a community advocate and provided immigration advice, dealt with marital matters and helped complete legal forms for those less literate in the community.

When my son started nursery, my husband encouraged me to go back to studying, so I went back to college and did my A levels and then went to university and got my accountancy qualification. When I was growing up, my father had an Asian grocery store called The Spice Box, where I was always his bookkeeper. Even after I was married, I was still doing my dad's books, so I thought, why don't I formalise it and do something in that field. Fortunately, it also opened up doors to other things.

After I finished my studies, it was hard to get a job at first, so I looked into volunteering. I was told about an organisation called Bawso, which helps BME victims of domestic abuse and other forms of violence against women. They were especially keen for people who could speak a second language to help interpret. The first person I met there was the finance officer, who was somebody I'd been studying with, so I volunteered for her in the financial department and loved it.

As soon as I had a bit of experience, I was able to get a job with one of the railway companies in their finance department. I was there for about three years, but I kept wishing I'd had a job in Bawso. I had a sense of belonging to the organisation because it's about gender equality and

Samsunear promoting Bawso, as the chosen charity for the Halal Food Festival in Cardiff, 2019

looking out for women's vulnerability. Given my experience of how I grew up and what my life could have been if I hadn't married, I felt I was in a position where I could influence and help other women and make changes.

In 2000, the Bawso finance officer post became vacant, and I applied for the role, was successful, and have been there ever since. Although my main role was finance, I was always part of developing new services. And while I'd been volunteering, I ventured into other areas purely out of interest. I worked in the refuge, provided child care, interpreted for women and participated in the 24-hour helpline, so I felt like I understood every part of the organisation. I've also got personal experience with family members who've gone through domestic abuse and forced marriage, and so on, so I think these subjects are very close to my heart. A lot of us in Bawso feel the same way, and it's not a 9 to 5 job for us. We will go beyond our remit of work, and with our experience and knowledge, we want to carry on making changes and helping others.

For the past ten years, I've been the deputy chief executive of Bawso and have been managing other projects, like volunteering, interpreting, HR and health and safety. I've also done a lot of commissioning of local authority services, even representing Bawso in the Welsh Government, by sitting on various strategic groups and trying to influence government policy. For example, Bawso was instrumental in propelling the 2015 Violence Against Women Domestic Abuse Sexual Violence Act. My passion for gender equality and women's rights drives me. One of my biggest challenges is trying to mainstream issues that affect the BME community, and I managed a project to do with FGM and forced marriage.

As a Bangladeshi Muslim woman, I think that I also have an opportunity of breaking down stereotypes, so I've found myself on various boards. I've been the chair of Minority Ethnic Women's Network Cymru and on the board of Race

Samsunear (*right*), running the Cardiff Half Marathon to fundraise for Bawso, 2016

Council Cymru and been involved with a lot of third-sector organisations, just to give my input from a BME perspective. I was also involved with the last couple of local council elections as a candidate for one of the parties, which was a good experience to see the political side of life and being involved with politicians and to influence ourselves on that platform too.

I do feel apprehensive about what's going on with racism and Islamophobia at the moment, especially when I'm walking around, wondering if I'm going to get mugged or if someone is going to question or challenge me. When I'm sitting on public transport, usually no one will sit next to me unless the whole place is full, which is why I prefer to drive because I feel safer in my own space. Naturally, people don't know who I am, what I do for a living or what I stand for. But I think no matter who I am, how confident I feel and what work I do for our community, to the wider society, I'm still a Bangladeshi Muslim woman who probably can't speak any English. So, I think those challenges still remain in the wider context, but I believe the work that I do will help to create social change and to push the boundaries of cultural norms in our society.

My ultimate goal is to influence change in a global setting. At present, being a mother and a carer, I'm constrained to helping at the national level, but one day, I would like to get involved with an international organisation so I can travel to other developing countries. Even if I don't achieve this goal, I hope I will have influenced my daughter, Numa, to take those next steps.

I've always tried to get my children involved in my work, fundraising or campaigning. My daughter played an active role in the school, helping other children with issues like

Samsunear with her daughter, Numa, at a Cardiff Muslim Primary School fundraiser, as the trustee board's treasurer, 2016

SEVENTY YEARS OF STRUGGLE AND ACHIEVEMENT 49

cyberbullying or domestic abuse, and in high school, she was given an Inspire anti-bullying award by the council. As an economics student at the university, she has secured a placement with an international pharmaceutical company and is planning to go to Zambia on a summer placement to train young people about sexual health.

I want my daughter to excel and go far and believe she can do it, and know that she has my support. I also have two sons, and my husband and I ensured that they were brought up learning about gender equality and shared roles and responsibility. I believe in practising what I preach.

I don't believe anybody else can make you happy. You have to make yourself happy and to be able to achieve. I think it's about challenging yourself, following your dream, and as long as you're not doing anything bad, don't let other people put boundaries within your life. I think I'm fortunate enough to have been able to have a relationship with my husband that left me free to think beyond our home and more about the world.

# Joyful Giving

## Poranee James
**CHAIPATTANA FOUNDATION VOLUNTEER AND COMMUNITY VOLUNTEER WORKER**

*In my view, everybody is equal, and each of us is brought into this world for the purpose of helping one another. To help people in trouble is most rewarding, and when I can do something for somebody, it gives me an immediate sense of pleasure and happiness in my heart.*

Poranee with her mother, sister and brother

I was born in Bangkok, Thailand, the eldest of three children. I enjoyed my childhood very much. I had a very privileged upbringing, with many people working for us at home, but we regarded them as sisters and brothers. This taught me to treat everybody as equal.

As a child, apart from my full-time education, I regularly attended Thai classical dance lessons at the most famous private dance school, and as I grew up, I was instructed by the same teachers. When I was ten or eleven years old, the group which I was a member of became quite famous in their own right. We regularly performed on Thai television all the time, and as we grew older, our individual and group pictures lined the wall at Thai Television's Channel 4. Our teachers would take us to dance at charity events, such as the Red Cross. These events were always attended by the King and Queen, so we performed dances for them too.

When I was eighteen, I came to the UK to study commerce and languages. I worked hard, and the principal was really pleased with me. At weekends, I would go travelling, joining tours to different cities. My parents encouraged me in this endeavour because they said, 'Travel is the best form of education', and through this, I developed a greater understanding of people from different cultures and backgrounds.

I came to the UK with three childhood friends from Thailand, but we attended different private colleges. On one occasion, the four of us decided to meet up and join a month-long tour that included visiting nine European countries. It was on this tour that I met my husband, who was a schoolteacher in Wales.

Fortunately, the group had become like family, and I remember at the end of the tour, on the coach, we all exchanged addresses. It was only many years after we were married that my husband told me that he went round the coach for one address only, as he did not want me to suspect anything. He was very reserved and remains so, even to this day. On my return to Thailand, he wrote letters to me from Wales twice a week, every Sunday and Wednesday, telling me about the pupils in his class and his family. He never once missed writing in this fashion.

After returning to Bangkok, I worked for the United Nations Economic and Social Commission for Asia and the Pacific. I was able to return to the UK every year to visit different friends, but I never went to Wales. After seven years, my future husband suggested I visit his parents and family who lived in a small seaside village while he was teaching elsewhere. I found, and still do that Welsh people are very much like Thai people because of their friendliness and welcoming nature and spirit. My future husband waited three more years for me because it was so difficult for me to make the final decision to get married, but finally, when I was 29 years old, I informed my mum that I was going to get married and settle down as a housewife. My mum laughed hilariously and told me that I would be dragging everybody out travelling again, and she was so right. I dragged my husband out to travel all the time.

For three whole months prior to our marriage, and while trying to decide where to live, I was very busy attending different events in Bangkok. It was a necessity to attend all events to avoid causing offence, and my social life was constantly hectic. However, here in the UK, one can decline an invitation without causing any offence. I also wanted to spend my life as an independent person, being able to do my own shopping, ironing, using public transport and being

Poranee in front of the United Nations building in Bangkok where she worked from 1967–1976

able to wear what I wanted. So, in the end, I decided the UK would be better, being much calmer and quieter for married life and for bringing up children.

It was seven years after our marriage that our son was born. I wanted to make sure everything was right and in place before I made the very big decision of bringing a child into the world. This was a big responsibility and needed very careful thinking and planning. As our son grew up, we let him decide which religious faith he wanted to follow. He attended a private Christian school and was, and still is, a gifted scholar and musician.

My charity work began when I was in Thailand. At weekends, I would go with my parents to visit such places as children's homes and the hospital for wounded soldiers. I also supported the Girl Guides Association in every way, both in funding and helping to teach.

Poranee with her husband and son, upon being presented with an honour for her voluntary work from the Thai King, Royal Thai Embassy, 2010

In Wales, I continued my charitable activities, beginning with the local church. On fundraising days, I made cakes and went to help. Even today, I continue to help many charities, including temples. I've had many opportunities to return to Thailand to be active in the Chaipattana Foundation, teaching English in a variety of schools. Here in Wales, I also helped find a location and supported the legal and financial requirements to set up the first Buddhist temple in Wales in a building in Rhymney, purchased by the Thai Government.

I've also had several people who have fled individual oppression in their own countries staying with us in our home. Fortunately, they were able to return to their homeland, except for one gentleman who fled from Tiananmen Square and now resides in the USA. He still keeps in touch with us, and to this day, calls us his Welsh Family. Such opportunities gave me a sense of complete contentment through being able to share, care and to help and support. What I do for people makes me happier each and every day of my life.

I was also fortunate to be able to set up the Thai Cultural Association of Wales and took up as chair of the organisation. This began when I used to arrange for Buddhist monks to attend religious events in Swansea three times a year. The monks would chant, preach, give a sermon and afterwards, all those assembled would gather, and after the monks had taken their meal, everyone would eat all the food that had been brought by the Thai volunteers. We were like a family.

The more I organised such events, the more people

Members of the Thai Cultural Association upon being awarded for being one of the best ten projects by the Wales Council for Voluntary Action

For several of the events, I arranged for the presence of a Thai classical orchestra, originally set up by Her Royal Highness Princess Maha Chakri Sirindhorn, as well as performances of seven dances, both classical and folk. The audience dined upon seven different dishes of food, and each guest, at the end of the event, received a Thai souvenir to take home with them. Every year, a different souvenir would be given, such as a key ring for the men and a small purse for the women. The event was a wonderfully successful community gathering, enabling people to come together. On one occasion, there were 36 different nationalities in attendance, totalling almost 500 guests.

If someone states that 'so and so is racist', I would tell them to come and visit our events. On doing so, one would not feel that at all because it has never mattered what came, from such places as Bristol, Newport, Abergavenny, Cwmbran, London, and other parts of the UK. After three or four years, I had to move the event to a larger venue to enable me to cater for 300 people from all walks of life and cultural backgrounds. The response and support from everyone were truly overwhelming, and I just couldn't believe it.

I also used to organise an annual Thai cultural event, usually held at the Brangwyn Hall in Swansea. This would take me an entire year to successfully organise, alongside my being in full-time employment as an assistant director of a global training organisation for journalists and broadcasters. But everyone enjoyed the event and were very willing to come and help.

Poranee at the Dylan Thomas Centre with members of a Thai dance group that she taught and performed with each year at the Brangwyn Hall in Swansea

ethnic background one was from or what position one held. Everybody is equal, and everyone at these events works well together, which remains so wonderful, even today.

Nobody can choose where or how one is born, what culture one is born into or whether one is rich or poor. I believe we are brought into this world for the purpose of helping one another. That's what I have always been taught and continue to do, even to this day.

Nowadays, I continue to be extremely busy and am fortunate that I never appear to tire. I do my best for today and tomorrow, wherever and whenever I can help somebody. I tell people not to worry and am able to help them through their difficult times. In doing these things and sharing, I am rewarded with total contentment because to me, one has to part with things anyway when one dies, so I may as well see somebody else having pleasure and being happy from the things I am able to share.

My husband and I think the same way in such matters. It appears to us both that holding onto money and not sharing things causes more problems than pleasure. One should be contented with what one has and with oneself, and then the remainder used to help people who are disadvantaged or less fortunate. Such ideals have been my guidelines throughout my life.

My husband and I have been married for 45 years. As I look back, I don't think my life has been anything but happy. My life's goal has always been to learn how to identify the source of any problems and how to overcome them for others. When I am able to do something to help someone, my reward is immediate happiness and joy within my heart. That, I believe, is true fulfilment in life.

# A Place of Refuge

## Chetna Sinha
**IMMIGRATION LAWYER, CHETNA AND CO SOLICITORS**

*I welcome anyone in vulnerable situations because many of them are suffering and need someone to talk to with a legal background who can give them some kind of reassurance. It's better if you can share your education and your knowledge, so you can see that everybody's doing well.*

Chetna as a student at Cardiff University, 1986

I was born and brought up in Bihar, India. My father was a lawyer, and my mum was a teacher, and I had four siblings. I was in India until I was 24. I came to Cardiff, where my uncles were and did my MSc in chemistry at Cardiff University. I went back to India a few years later, in 1988, and got married to a man called Santosh Kumar. After a few years, we moved to Delhi. I have two boys, Gautam Narayan and Kanishka Narayan.

Although I did a Master's degree in science, I realised this career was not going to get me anywhere, and I changed my mind. I was working in the Delhi High Courts, and I decided to train as a lawyer. There were many lawyers in the family, including my father and grandfather, so I was a bit influenced by them. I thought I could work for myself and be my own boss, as I never wanted to work for anybody else. I also thought if I do it on my own, I could look after my family the way I would like to. So I decided to train as a lawyer, and my father-in-law, who was also a lawyer and a lecturer at the law college, supported and helped me. So that's how I became a lawyer.

I didn't practise law straight away because of my kids. I wanted my boys to be a little independent before I left home. When Gautam was at school full-time, I started my practice at the Delhi High Court. For the first few years, I worked with two different firms, doing environmental and corporate law, and then I started my own firm, which was wonderful. But when my uncles from Cardiff came to visit me, they kept pressuring me to come back to Cardiff, saying

Chetna with husband, Santosh Kumar, at a Christmas party in Cardiff, 2018

I was working too hard. In Delhi, it's a very hard, fast life, running around all the time.

In 2000, one of the uncles, who I was very close to, passed away. The other uncle wanted us to come and stay with him so that he would have more family in Cardiff. So we came two years later, my boys being eleven and twelve at that point. I passed my solicitors' exam and got a job in a law firm.

Unfortunately, my boys were unhappy in Cardiff, and for the first few months, they felt out of place. They wanted to go back to Delhi, as they had left their childhood friends and what they knew. But we had always said that getting the best education is very important, so Kanishka applied and got a scholarship to go to boarding school. My elder son, Gautam, did medicine at Birmingham University, and we had to pay international fees for him.

Although both Santosh and I had qualified as solicitors, there were no job opportunities in Cardiff. At first, I volunteered and then managed to work as a junior lawyer in a couple of firms. Then I realised that starting my own firm would be possible and probably the best way for us to do some meaningful work. Immigration law made the most sense in terms of my language skills and the community network that I had. So I opened Chetna and Co Solicitors, and Santosh became my partner, and we're partners still. Our lives were unstable for some time, as we didn't know if we were going to be granted permanent residency, which takes a long time, but fortunately, it all worked out and around 2009, we got our residency. Kanishka went on to become an expert civil service adviser in Cameron's government and left when Brexit was passed. He's now doing an MBA at Stanford University in America.

I've been fortunate because Cardiff has given me so much. I've been educated and have worked here, and the city has been my second home, so I wanted to give something back to the community. In my work as a solicitor, I realised that there are many Asian people, especially women, that can't speak up, either because of language barriers or things they don't want to share with the British community. So as an immigration lawyer, I started a free surgery every Saturday from 10–2 for Asian women or any married women who had whatever kind of problem they wanted to discuss with me, and I would give them confidential advice.

Chetna with her husband and sons, Kanishka Narayan and Gautam Narayan, at Gautam's birthday party, 2017

I started advising many women, particularly those who were victims of domestic violence. There were many ladies who came from Pakistan, Bangladesh and even India whose passports were taken away from them. They used to work like slaves and manage all of the family's affairs and were not allowed to go out or even given proper food. They were on temporary visas and worried that their domestic situation would affect their visa status. So I would advise them, as well as women who had fled a situation of persecution or abuse abroad and were seeking to file for asylum in the UK. Every Saturday, I used to teach my clients' kids as well, and Gautam and Kanishka used to help me too. We did this for a number of years.

I was also the chair of Bawso (Black Association of Women Step Out) for nearly six years and am still a member. In 2011, I was nominated for a WAWAA award for social and humanitarian work, and I won the prize. It was a happy moment for me but unexpected because although I like to help, I never thought I had done that much for the community. My jobs are quite hidden, and I don't like to expose myself or say I've done this or that.

I'm still helping people, like asylum seekers from Syria or whoever is coming through, just to give them the confidence that they are in a safe place and what they should do. I welcome anyone in vulnerable situations to come and talk, without an appointment, because they need someone to talk to them with a legal background who can give them some kind of reassurance. Many of them are suffering, so I help get them to a refugee centre or whatever I can do. It's better if you can share your education and your knowledge, so you can see that everybody's doing well.

# Self-belief

# Future Potentials

## Meena Upadhyaya
**MEDICAL GENETICIST AND PROFESSOR, FOUNDER AND CHAIR OF EMWWAA AND EMWWH**

*My philosophy is that life is full of challenges, but you shouldn't be put off by them, but rather to do your best and never give up. And by accepting challenges, you become a more compassionate and resilient person.*

I was born in India, one of six children. My mother was a housewife, and my father was an astute mechanical and electrical engineer, and later on, an accomplished businessman. Discipline and traditional values were instilled in me during my upbringing. I was sent to Queen Mary's School, a girls' public school in Delhi, but as a mission school, it was in contrast to my conservative Brahman family's ideology. Being a boarder at this international school was a wonderful experience, and I met many interesting girls from various countries. It was the perfect forum for forging friendships and developing a young mind with a diverse outlook. I was the head girl at the boarding house and a senior prefect in the school, so I learned to accept and embrace responsibilities and appreciate diversity at an early age.

Following my higher secondary education, I joined a renowned college, Miranda House, at Delhi University and obtained a science degree. While at university, I got married through an arranged marriage. I was the first student in my year to get married, and it was attended by

Meena, (*standing, third from the right*) participating in a Gazal programme at the Queen Mary's School, Delhi

SEVENTY YEARS OF STRUGGLE AND ACHIEVEMENT

all my classmates, and they had a blast. My husband, Krishna, was a student at Edinburgh University and was visiting his parents at the time. As was traditional at the time, I saw my husband for the first time during our wedding, though he had seen me before from afar.

Meena as a bride in Modinagar, India

After our marriage, I stayed in India to finish my studies and later joined Krishna in Edinburgh, where he had now found a job. When I came to the UK, I had no ambitions whatsoever and thought I would follow the footsteps of my older sisters, who were very proud to be housewives. But I found in Edinburgh that I was bored and lonely sitting at home listening to Bollywood music while Krishna went to work. I was used to the hustle and bustle of India and my busy college life, and was also pretty homesick. I was mesmerised by the department stores and expressed a desire to work in one of them.

My request was instantly denied by Krishna, as it was not the done thing at the time for women in my family to work. He suggested I join the university for further studies, so I enrolled at Edinburgh University. Initially, it was for a PhD in Animal Genetics, but when I realised I was pregnant with my daughter, I shifted to doing an MSc, which I was able to complete after she was born. The birth of my lovely daughter was one of the happiest moments of my life.

I then joined Krishna, who was transferred to Cardiff, and here I was able to spend quality time with my daughter, regularly feeding ducks at the Roath Park and watching her grow and blossom. I soon realised that I was not cut out to sit at home, so once my daughter started school, I joined the Welsh National School of Medicine to pursue a PhD in Male Infertility in the Department of Obstetrics and Gynaecology. Every day I would drop my daughter at school and focus diligently on my lab-based research, and then collect her from school at 3.30pm, and we'd watch *Blue Peter* together after she had been fed. Those were some

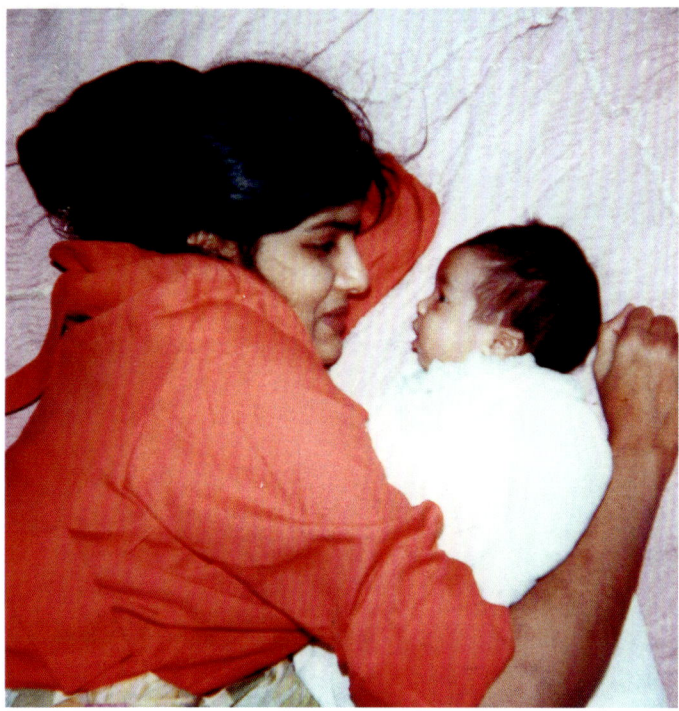

Meena trying to make conversation with her 3-month-old daughter, Rachna

lovely and wonderful times that created deeply fond memories. I did, however, have a rigorous schedule. My husband would return from work around 6pm, and I would go back to my lab to finish the rest of my experiments for the day. It was quite a challenging time, but we managed between the two of us, and we were a happy little family.

Very unexpectedly, the first week I started writing my thesis, my husband died suddenly of a massive heart attack. This was a huge shock to me, as there had been no indication of any illness. His death ended up changing the world completely for me and my young daughter. While grieving, not only did I have to think about my studies, but also bringing up my daughter as a single parent in a country that was still somewhat foreign to me. Unfortunately, the rest of my family was back in India, so I didn't have any family support here. Some of my family members did visit me from India to provide some support, but they could only stay here for a short period and tried to persuade us to return to India where we would be well looked after and supported. However, that was not an option for me, as I wanted to finish writing my thesis, and my young daughter was not too keen to move to India, as her friends were in Cardiff.

We simply carried on, though it was a complete nightmare. I had lost a stone in weight within six months. I had depended on Krishna in many ways; for instance, I had not paid any utility bills, I could drive the car, but I had not dealt with road tax, MOT, and insurance. I couldn't work on my thesis for at least a year, as I was still in shock and suffering from grief and depression and the gravity of facing my future, and was close to a nervous breakdown. I am grateful to many of my kind and caring friends for their support in this difficult time. After much determination and willpower, I made an effort to resume writing my thesis, as I realised it was important to complete it so I could provide the support for my daughter that she deserved. Following extensive labour, resolve, and time management, I was finally awarded my PhD.

I was then offered a job as a post-doctorate research fellow at the Institute of Medical Genetics at Cardiff

University. My first research project was on prenatal diagnosis in the first trimester for genetic conditions. This was a very exciting project because before this, women had to wait until sixteen weeks of pregnancy to have a test

Lamp lighting ceremony at the first international Rasopathy conference in Asia, organised by Meena at Kochi, Kerala, India in 2017

done, whereas this test could be done between eight and twelve weeks. Prior to these tests, many women with serious hereditary conditions in their families chose not to have children, so these tests empowered women and their partners to make their own reproductive choices. This pioneering work was published in the high-profile journal, *The Lancet*.

At this stage, I found my research work therapeutic as it diverted me from my ongoing grief. I pay tribute to my late mentor Professor Sir Peter Harper, who sadly died in 2021. His belief in me and my research, and his encouragement to succeed had a lasting effect on me. I endeavour to transmit the knowledge and experience I acquired from him to my students.

I then became involved in the mapping and cloning of disease genes. Of many diseases I have conducted research on, one of them, Neurofibromatosis type 1 (NF1), a familial cancer syndrome, became very close to my heart, and my research findings were acknowledged globally. The most fulfilling part of my career was meeting with patients and their families to reassure them that we were doing our best to find a treatment for their disease through our research. I am still in touch with many NF1 Welsh families, and I am a trustee as well as on the Medical Advisory Committee for Nerve Tumours UK (a national charity that provides support to patients with nerve tumours).

Leading genetic research and development required me to stay well versed in all the new genetic developments. My longest work time spent outside Cardiff included my visit to the Howard Hughes Institute at the Salt Lake City, USA for five weeks to learn cutting-edge technology, and a month at Tokai University Medical College, Japan, to learn a novel technique called laser-capture microdissection. I have travelled widely, presenting my research findings. My international collaborations allowed me to interact with diverse minds and gave me great purpose and direction in life. I was the first female British Indian Professor in Medical Genetics in the UK.

However, as I gradually rose in ranks through hard work and considerable self-sacrifice over the years, it meant forgoing holidays and other personal time with my growing daughter. Like many women, balancing family life with professional life was always taxing, and I still feel very guilty when I think about my time away from my growing daughter for work and missing some of her milestone birthdays. Despite these misgivings, I am very proud that my daughter qualified as a medical doctor, and later went on to graduate with an MBA from Imperial College, London, and excelled in pharmaceutical investment research in London, and she has always considered me to be her role model. I am now a proud and happy grandmother, and my eleven-year-old granddaughter has become my lifeline.

As a BME immigrant, I had to work twice as hard, if not more, to be recognised, and I encountered many barriers at work and beyond because of my language, culture, appearance and religion. I faced both racial and gender discrimination and developed coping strategies to internalise hurt, though I'm also fortunate to have found some understanding, and caring colleagues in my life. I've come to realise that integration can be a very powerful factor. I'm very proud to be a British Indian, and it has been an enriching experience for me to have developed my career in Wales.

I'm also very proud of my country of origin and its culture. I have been inspired by my grandparents, who were freedom fighters and ended up as political prisoners, like Mahatma Gandhi. My grandmother Premkala Dwivedi was an exceptional woman of her time; she was awarded 'Tamra Patra' by the Prime minister of India, Indira Gandhi, in 1972 at 25th anniversary ceremony of India's independence for her campaign for freedom.

In 2008, I was nominated for a Welsh Women of the Year award, and although I didn't get the award, when I looked around and saw there were hardly any BME women in the crowd, I thought, wouldn't it be nice to have an awards ceremony just for BME women? A couple of years later, I began working on setting up such an organisation; I was much encouraged by Julie Morgan, MP. Having no experience in the charity sector, I was fortunate to meet up with some like-minded women from India, Pakistan, Bangladesh, Nepal, and Sri Lanka who helped put it all together. The first ceremony was for Asian women and has since expanded and is known as the Ethnic Minority Welsh Women Achievement Association (EMWWAA).

Many amazing BME women struggle and do not get an opportunity to reach their full potential. EMWWAA is the

Meena with the finalists at the EMWWAA Awards ceremony, 2019

only organisation in Wales that specifically empowers and acknowledges BME women and girls and identifies role models from different communities, while also promoting cohesion and integration. The organisation thus makes a difference in many BME women's lives and offers inspiration to countless numbers of people.

It was also a great pleasure for me to launch the Ethnic Minority Women in Welsh Healthcare (EMWWH) in 2015. While BME women make up a significant proportion of health and care workers, they are markedly under-represented in leadership positions. EMWWH aims to connect BME women in healthcare in Wales and to create a supportive and empowering network that promotes equality and diversity. I feel we have to continue with our efforts to empower, educate, promote and build the confidence of BME women and girls.

I extend my gratitude to to Wales and the UK governments for awarding me many accolades, way beyond my expectations, such as an Inspire Wales award, a St David award and an OBE for my contribution to science and the community. Currently, I am a council member for the Royal College of Pathologists and the Learned Society of Wales. I have also been decorated with a European Theodore Schwann award and was recently appointed to the role of a non-executive director on the Welsh Government Civil Service Board.

It has been a very challenging but worthwhile journey for me. I particularly missed not having had a BME role model when I encountered multiple obstacles in my life; as such

Meena receiving an OBE at Buckingham Palace, 2016

women were in short supply. It is gratifying that EMWWAA and EMWWH continue to identify many aspiring role models and I am much inspired by these truly remarkable women. Life is full of challenges, but I believe you shouldn't be put off by them, but rather do your best, and never give up. By accepting challenges, you become a more resilient and compassionate person. When I look back on all the challenges I faced, I would never have imagined that not only I would move up in my chosen career, but also manage to help women to gain recognition for their achievements, despite the many obstacles they continue to face. My resounding message to women everywhere is not to give up. Or, as Nelson Mandela once said so inspirationally, 'It always seems impossible until it's done.'

# Learning Curves

## Chantal Patel
**HEAD OF INTERPROFESSIONAL HEALTH STUDIES AT THE COLLEGE OF HUMAN & HEALTH SCIENCES, SWANSEA UNIVERSITY**

*I encourage people to think outside the box, and for those who feel they're not ready, I always say to them that there's no harm in trying. It doesn't matter how long it takes you to get where you need to go, as long as you map your journey and do everything that will help you to get to that particular point.*

I was born in Mauritius, at a time when the country was very unspoiled with hardly any tourists. I was brought up with five other siblings in a very strict Roman Catholic family, and it was challenging having to conform to what was expected from both a parental and societal perspective. I considered myself a free spirit with a childlike curiosity, hungry for new information and experiences.

I went to a private convent school run by nuns, which was very strict, but I received a good level of education, which I only appreciated later on in life. I was very interested in arts and drama, as well as sports, particularly hurdles, long jump and volleyball, but I had to do these things without my parents' knowledge or approval. They would not have agreed to let me take part, as they didn't see any value in such things and were of the view that I had to put my head down and study and get good grades.

But as a child, I was quite willing to break the rules and do things I knew my parents wouldn't have accepted. By the time I was a teenager, I knew that I wanted to get out of the restrictive, religious environment. I questioned the whole notion of religion, which did not sit well with the nuns who ran the school. I felt that I wouldn't have had the freedom to do the things I wanted to do because my parents would have wanted me to marry or to do a job that they wanted me to do, so I felt quite hemmed in.

It was pure luck that one day in 1974 when I was eighteen, I was mitching from school and went with friends to the capital to a large nursing recruitment event, where they were looking for people to undertake nursing studies in the UK for a period of five years. Several months later, I was accepted to the programme, and within a few weeks of receiving the acceptance letter, I was off to the UK, so my parents didn't have much time to think about it.

Fortunately, a couple of uncles supported my decision,

claiming that this was a golden opportunity. There weren't many jobs going in Mauritius, and I didn't want to be married off to a European man, as many of my peers had been. I was happy I'd been given this ticket to freedom, though I didn't know where I'd be going or how I was going to communicate.

I ended up in Bridgend, though I'd never even heard of Wales. On arrival, it was a cultural shock, and for someone who couldn't stop talking, I found myself almost unable to communicate the way that I was accustomed to. Within a week of arriving, I was inducted into the School of Nursing, which was a further shock, but I felt lucky to be supported by my peers on the nursing programme, who were fabulous.

I recall how our nursing lecturers spoke so fast that I had no idea what they were saying, and it got so bad that I had to walk around with a dictionary. I was kind of surviving from day to day and developing a lot of non-verbal cues of watching other people and trying to interpret what was going on around me. I knew that I had to take steps to improve my English, so I went to evening school, where I met lots of others who were looking to improve their English. I was missing all the activities I had undertaken in Mauritius and found an advertisement in the local paper for anyone interested in playing volleyball at a newly established club. I went along and fitted in very quickly, having played volleyball since the age of eleven. I also made some lifelong friends there.

By the second year of the nursing course, I discovered that I understood very quickly what to do and was good at it, despite not having had any background in looking after anyone for any length of time. Though I had fully embraced the caring side of me, I was quite taken aback when I was awarded a prize for the best medical student nurse. I later studied mental health nursing for eighteen months. Though I learned a lot, I ultimately found that this wasn't for me because you have to be a very relaxed and self-reflective kind of person to nurse patients with mental illnesses. That said, it did give me an insight into mental distress that has remained with me to this day. I returned to general nursing and had an opportunity to go onto an orthopaedic surgical ward. Soon after, I was appointed a ward sister and was one of the youngest ones in this role, and from an ethnic background too, which was quite rare.

I was very creative as a ward sister and also discovered that I had an aptitude for management. We did a lot of fundraising in order to buy things for patients, and I think we were the first orthopaedic ward in Wales to have duvets, which were less constrictive for these patients than the usual bed sheets and blankets. We worked very hard and had a tremendous rapport with our patients. Back then, we had a lot more freedom as nurses with regards to managing our shift patterns and covering for each other. We became like a family, celebrating each others' birthdays and going on outings together to places like London and Ladies' Day at Ascot.

Chantal (*back, second from the right*), as a member of the Bridgend Volleyball Club, participating in a volleyball tournament in Wales, 1984

Chantal (*right*) with two walking buddies, hiking 26 miles to raise money for Macmillan Cancer Support, 2017

Chantal with her husband, Gokul and their children, Michael, Alex and Beini, Christmas, 2017

By this time, I had married my husband, who I had met when he was a medical student in Cardiff. He was born in India but was brought up in London. In 1985, I'd been offered a manager's post but soon discovered I was pregnant. I decided that I didn't want to take the post for just nine months, and in fact, I had made up my mind to give up nursing completely once my baby was born because I didn't have any family support.

My husband got his first practice in Swansea, and we moved there, and I found myself on an estate where I didn't know anyone. After my son was born, I went to baby and toddler groups, and over a period of time, met people who had common interests. But I knew that staying at home and looking after children would not be sufficient, so I decided to do a law degree at what was then the Swansea Institute of Higher Education. I did my degree in three years, despite having two young children by then. I went into legal practice but wasn't there for very long because I realised as a solicitor, a lot of the work you do is in an office on your own, which was not for me.

At that time, the Swansea Institute was setting up a law school and were looking for lecturers to teach on its accredited programme. So, after I obtained my PGCE, I taught land and employment law, and when the Institute merged with Swansea University, I began teaching applied medical law. This gave me a chance to put to good use all the things I'd learnt when I was a nurse, and teaching applied law to a whole group of different healthcare professionals broadened my horizon in terms of those disciplines. I had very good colleagues who were very supportive and mentored me without me realising I was being mentored.

In 2006, I became the head of the department for Interprofessional Studies at Swansea University, looking after all kinds of healthcare programmes. It's been a really good learning environment for me because I'm constantly learning something new. I've also sat on boards like the Swansea Bay University Health Board, Gower College and the Gwalia Housing Trust (now Pobl). In 2018, I was appointed the UNESCO chair for Bioethics, which enabled me to present papers at their international conferences. I have a particular interest in the ethics of organ transplantation, and at the college, I helped set up a centre for this. I also helped establish the Family Glamorgan Development Centre in Swansea, which enables estranged parents to reconnect with their children and to support large numbers of families over a long period of time. I'm very proud of that charity, and it's taught me a lot as well.

Culturally, I have always been interested in community activities. I was the secretary of the Indian Society for nearly seven years, and to this day, I am still a trustee. I'm also one of the founding members of the African Community Centre, led by Professor Uzo Iwobi, a place that has made me recognise the plight of people fleeing persecution and economic ruin.

I've seen my life as an adventure but also had to learn many things quickly without having an opportunity to sit back and think if this was the road I wanted to go down. I've also had many challenges, being from an ethnic minority, particularly from people who didn't want to rent properties to me. Also, professionally, as a female in the 1970s, there were a lot of comments about why I would want a particular job when I was not the main breadwinner. Despite this, I never gave up and truly believed in the motto: 'What is meant to be will always find its way.'

So my journey has really been a huge learning curve about my fellow humans and things that I can do in the workplace. For example, I never think that I know enough and always think that I can learn more from people, like my students. I do have people come to me, and they say they're inspired by me, which pleases me because I think I must be doing something right. I encourage people to think outside the box, and for those who feel they're not ready, I always say to them that there's no harm in trying. Even if you don't succeed the first time, there's always going to be another opportunity. So if you fall, pick yourself up and do it again because next time, the experience may well be different.

It's how you perceive yourself that is really important. It doesn't matter how long it takes you to get where you

Chantal receiving an EMWWAA Lifetime Achievement award, 2017

need to go, as long as you map your journey and do everything that will help you to get to that particular point. That's not to say that it's going to be an easy road because you will find many obstacles along the way, but what I would say to people, as well as to my younger self, is that when faced with challenges, you're stronger than you think.

And you won't always have parents who will support you, but this is where I see the beauty of community groups because these are people who are going to give you the confidence to go beyond your boundaries and help you to flourish. You also need to be as curious as you can. Keep asking those questions, and then make up your own mind along the way. It's also important to not lose sight of your dreams and realise that everything happens for a reason.

There are still many things I'd like to do in the future,

especially once I've retired from my day job. I have many ideas for books and articles, which I hope to publish. I'd also like to learn new languages and am currently learning Welsh and Russian. I'd also like to do a degree in psychology. In my mind, I still feel like a thirty-year-old, so I'm kind of looking forward to the next chapter. It'll be interesting to see what happens.

# Game Changing

## Gaynor Legall
**CHAIRPERSON AT THE HERITAGE & CULTURAL EXCHANGE**

*Before you try and break the rules, learn the rules of the game well, and then you can try and make changes. It's also important to have a belief in yourself that you can do it, but you have to learn to be good at what you're doing.*

I was born in Cardiff and grew up in Butetown. I have one brother, but as my mother was a foster mother, there were always lots of other children and people coming in and out of the house. I had a very happy, privileged childhood because, although we were very poor in economic terms, we were very rich in friendships and support, and I had exposure to different types of people, religion, and I felt love and protection.

I've always been interested in and wanting to do everything. I did ballet and tap dancing and read a lot; although we didn't have books or magazines in our house, I read everyone else's books. Growing up in Butetown, we would roam around in gangs all over the city. We would walk or cycle and, as there wasn't much room in the house to play, everyone played in the streets. Then when television came, I was a real telly addict and watched it as much as I could.

My Uncle Robert was a seaman, and when he was back home, he used to take me to meetings at the Seamen's Union. I was the type of child who could sit quietly with a book and listen to what was going on, so I heard lots of

Gaynor, age 4, with her brother, Alan

adults' conversations. This was in the 1960s, at a time when many Commonwealth countries were gaining their independence, so I listened to discussions about them. So as a child, I was quite politically aware, without understanding an awful lot about it.

My mother used to say that I was an interfering, bossy little girl, and I continued becoming an interfering, bossy woman. When I see things that I think are wrong or need to be improved, I have to restrain myself from getting in there and changing or improving them.

I got involved in community politics quite young. When I was eighteen, I met some people who'd been exiled from South Africa and were involved in the anti-apartheid movement, so I became part of the Wales anti-apartheid movement myself. I began to look more in-depth into politics and helped start an organisation called the Black Alliance. We copied some of the slogans and organisation from the Black Power movement in America but tempered it. We called it the Black Alliance, recognising that a lot of people from here are mixed-race or were married to or living with white partners.

Gaynor with members of the Anti-Racist Alliance (a successor to Anti-Apartheid Wales) at Butetown Carnival, c.1992

We wanted to teach Black children about their history and themselves, to give them some pride in who they were and where their parents came from. We were trying to widen the outlook of the young people from Butetown, to tell them that the whole city was theirs, and more of them should be going on to university and things like that. But we had a rough time. We were shunned by community leaders as troublemakers, and actually, the Butetown Community Centre committee banned us from using it. Even the police said we were militant thugs. I don't think they understood what we were talking about, and they didn't give us a chance to explain in any detail. They thought we were anti-white, but we weren't attacking white people. My grandmother was white, and she was a very important figure in my life, and there were white people in our organisation. They didn't understand what we meant by Black history, so they just saw us as a threat.

Then I got involved in welfare rights, with the Citizens Advice Bureau's housing sector and, also, trained and worked as a social worker. Then I decided I would stand as a city councillor for Butetown, which was an interesting time. People thought I was mad because part of my patch as a social worker was Butetown. As a social worker, I could go into homes and deal with quite difficult or complicated problems and see the same person in the shop later on, and they'd never acknowledge my role as a social worker. But as a councillor, the expectations were so high. I'd be going to the shop, or I'd be out at night dancing, and people would tell me about their housing problems.

During the time I was a councillor from 1979 to 1984, I ran a surgery on Thursday nights at the community centre for a couple of hours. There were queues of people, and they came from different parts of Cardiff as well. Because I was Black, they thought I would understand and help them more, and I would have to explain that they had to go and see their own councillor.

It was a really difficult time in terms of change for Butetown as well. There was a housing policy where they were trying to build more homeless shelters and were housing homeless people in a tower block. A lot of them had psychiatric problems, and they'd come and tell me the council had put an aerial in their head and were transmitting their thoughts. Some of these people had been living rough for years and didn't know how to cope with high-rise living and were not offered any support. So I used to see all of them as well, and it was just a real mixed bag.

When I was first elected, we were in opposition, and the Tories were in control, and in my second term, it was a hung parliament, so I had very little power or influence. I could only work if I could get other councillors on my side, and Butetown only had one councillor, which I think was wrong. It's a very complex area and even more so now. So I just got completely fed up with not being able to do anything, and after two terms, I stood down.

I had already taken up a new job, which meant I was travelling around Wales more, so it became too much anyway. My new job was as a team leader for the Ethnic Minorities Social Work Team, which was the first of its kind in Wales. It was made up of aspiring social workers who were Indian, Pakistani, African, and Central American, and the idea was that we would give service to minority ethnic people in a wide area of South Glamorgan. We basically dealt with everything and were sent anyone whose name

Gaynor, as the first director of the Afiya Trust, a BME-led organisation addressing issues in health and social care

sounded foreign. Most of the team were unqualified social workers, so it was about us all learning together until they eventually became qualified. It was an exciting time building the team up, and I enjoyed it.

Then I felt I needed to expand a bit and have a better salary, so I got a job as the assistant divisional director for Barnardo's. Our division was Wales and the South West of England, and we had a series of projects that worked with young homeless people, children and young people with disabilities, youth justice, families in crisis—the whole spectrum. We had projects spread all over the place, and we developed our responses to what the families needed. I loved the job, and what was interesting for me was working in different areas, which gave me a good perspective of Wales.

I met lots of members of the Royal Family via Barnardo's, including Princess Diana, who was a patron at the time. I also met Prince Charles when he visited an organisation I set up called Cardiff Inner-City Initiative, which was about helping and training young inner-city kids who'd been excluded from school. Then we merged and became New Employ, where I was a voluntary director. A lot of the people you see from Butetown, who are now in good jobs, started there.

Gaynor receiving an EMWWAA Lifetime Achievement award from the former First Minister of Wales, Rhodri Morgan, 2017.

I feel quite proud, and I know I've made a difference in quite a few people's lives, which is really rewarding. I get as much pleasure from seeing people achieve, rather than recognition for me doing anything, and I really enjoy playing a background role, getting things organised and set up. I love to see people fly and reach their potential. I think that if you've been given opportunities and chances, then you should give back as much as you can. That's just the way I've been brought up, and that's the way I think.

I wouldn't say I feel totally satisfied because there's always a sense looking back that you could have done more—hindsight is a wonderful thing, but you can't go back, so I have no regrets because they're pointless. I'm quite proud of what I've achieved, particularly given my start in life and where I came from, and how disadvantaged the area was in terms of education. I've always been confident, and I think the confidence has come from the people in my community and their voices. I feel comfortable with people and am not put off because somebody looks or speaks differently or has an accent. It doesn't faze me because that's how I grew up, so that's been a huge contributory factor.

I've also been very fortunate to have had an athletic career. I was always quite sporty, and I liked to run about. I really thrived at my secondary school, Grangetown Secondary Modern, and I became the sports' captain. I was a sprinter and ran for the school and then Cardiff, and was selected for the women's team for Wales in various sporting events and loved it. We went to different places for trials and games and often stayed overnight and were put up by local families. So I was meeting different people and seeing the way they lived, which was very different from the way I grew up and lived. I loved going on stage and getting the trophies and such. I just wish I'd trained harder and been doing it since because look at the money they make now!

I used to say to my team: 'Before you go in and try and break the rules, learn the rules of the game well, and then you can make changes, because you know you're going to be challenged, so you've got to be sure of what you're talking about.' It's important to have a belief in yourself that you can do it and to try. You have to learn to be good at what you're doing. As I say to my granddaughter, 'One step at a time, but practice makes perfect.'

# Spirited Storytelling

## Chandrika Joshi
**SPECIAL NEEDS DENTIST, PRIESTESS AND STORYTELLER**

*Life is a journey and not a destination. The universe gives you what you need, even if it does not give you what you want. The thing to do is keep an open heart and accept what comes your way as a blessing.*

I was born in a small village in Uganda called Iganga. My father was a Hindu priest and my mother was a homemaker, and we were a close family of six siblings living in a small house. My parents were middle class and did relatively well, so life was very secure and there wasn't a struggle for money, which was significant because education was not free. Fortunately, all of us excelled in our studies, particularly my older brother and sister.

I remember it always being sunny in the village, with rope swings hanging from beautiful mango trees. You could go running around barefoot exploring everything, from the forest, which was at the edge of the village, to the school to pick jasmine flowers and look at the vast variety of butterflies. I was very creative and used to love painting, drawing, writing and dancing. I also had a thread of spirituality from a young age and wanted to explore God, and questioned my parents about the philosophies around Hinduism.

Life changed for me when my father had a massive stroke in his 40s, which created an incredible upheaval in our lives. My mother moved into the hospital, which was in

Outside the primary school in Uganda, 1969. Chandrika is standing second from the left

another town called Jinja, to help take care of my father, and took my six-month-old baby brother with her. Five of us were left at home under the care of my twelve-year-old brother, Pankaj, and my ten-year-old sister took care of my two-year-old sister. I was seven at the time. Although the neighbours helped, it was a traumatic experience, and all my siblings and I were seared by this event in our lives.

My father was in a coma for the first week but woke up later with my amazing mother by his side. The right side of his body was paralysed and he couldn't move his limbs on that side. There were no physiotherapists, but as my mother was told that physiotherapy was the only hope, she exercised my father's limbs all day long while nursing a baby in tow. When my father was discharged, my mother, with the help of a neighbour's son, continued the physiotherapy at home until he was eventually able to walk. She also cut down the salt in his food, which he was unhappy about because he loved his food, but she tolerated his frustrations until he got used to the new diet. Once my father could walk again, he would go for miles and miles every day to maintain good health.

Uganda was a country with no social service support, so if you didn't earn money, you would starve. With my father being unwell, there was no income coming in, so my mother and older brother started learning from my father and conducting some parts of the priestly services. When my father was better, my mother returned to being a homemaker, and my father resumed working with the help of my older brother, Pankaj, whose life totally changed. At the age of twelve, he went from being a child to an adult in a flash. My siblings and I were in awe of Pankaj for what he did for our family and us.

I was fourteen when we had to leave Uganda. In August 1972, Idi Amin announced that he wanted Ugandan Asians with British passports to leave the country within three months. The whole fabric of society that we knew began to unravel and Uganda was totally turned upside down. Everyone was fending for themselves, and my father felt vulnerable because of his disability and didn't know what to do. He didn't want to split the family and, as my brother

Family photo, 1970. Chandrika is in the back on the left. Her brother, Pankaj, is seated on the right next to their parents

was already in the UK doing his A levels, he decided we should come here.

Logistically, it was very difficult to leave, and when my father managed to get plane tickets, we had less than 24 hours to pack our bags and leave. The journey was very difficult and especially traumatic, and we were relieved when we finally managed to get our seats on the plane. We landed in Heathrow in October, freezing in our summer clothes. A charity met us coming off the plane and gave us warm clothes and took us to a massive refugee camp at Tonfanau Army Barracks in north Wales. I remember leaving the train station and being in this wilderness in the rain, with sheep climbing the hills and the smell of salt and seaweed in the air.

We were at the refugee camp for four months, where my sister sat her O level exams and I went to the local school in Tywyn. Life in the camp was stressful because I came from a small, conservative village and felt exposed in this unstable environment. We also lost our family stability because my mother suddenly became very ill with a heart infection. She was taken to a hospital in Machynlleth. It was difficult for any of us to visit her, and my mother, being so isolated and worried about us, had a nervous breakdown.

In February 1973, my family was finally given a little council estate house in a village called Penrhys in the Rhondda, and my mother came home a week later. The Rhondda people were lovely—very friendly and nosy, which is very helpful for refugees, especially my father, who was disabled and my mum with her poor heart. There were ten refugee families in a similar situation to us who were housed in the Rhondda in different villages, so we started mingling with them. I can understand how minority groups in this country stick to their culture more strongly than in their homeland, because you want so much not to erase who you are and where you come from.

I went through a journey over the next four or five years that was really difficult for me on a personal level, trying to fit in and arguing with my parents all the time. I passed thirteen O levels but totally failed my A levels. In retrospect, I was probably suffering from depression, feeling lonely and isolated. I applied to do radiotherapy in Middlesex Hospital in London, going from a little village to central London, with my social phobia and lack of self-confidence. I had to resit my physics exam, and they decided to kick me out of the course, saying I wasn't bright enough for radiography.

I came to Cardiff and couldn't find anything to do because I was considered too bright for certain things and not bright enough for others, and there was no middle ground for me. Finally, I got onto a new course started by the Welsh Office called Physiological Measurements, and that's when I vowed that I would prove to myself that I could do anything I put my mind to. I was lucky I had a mentor called Carol Jones, who believed in me and encouraged me to fly high. She was like a fairy godmother or guardian angel, and everyone needs that.

I started studying really hard right from the beginning and got distinctions in every exam I sat, and was awarded a prize by the Welsh Office. I wanted to go to university, and I applied to do dentistry, thinking I might not be bright

Chandrika officiating as a priestess at a wedding in Perth

enough for medicine. However, dentistry has been a fantastic career for me. I work as a specialist in special care dentistry two days a week. I work only with special needs patients—people with various impairments—mental, physical or medical, meaning that they can't access the general dental service.

Another avenue I've pursued is as a Hindu priestess. Once my father resumed working as a priest, he used to take one of the children with him to help. It was usually my older brother who went with him, but we younger ones also had a chance, and it was such an honour to be by his side learning and listening. I would sit by him, always very nervous because my father was very strict, very methodical, and a perfectionist.

In 2002, a young man I knew from Uganda was getting married to an English girl. My father had conducted the marriage of his parents and he wanted someone from our family to do his wedding, and I offered to do it. I sat down and started learning the service, and my first wedding was in Leicester, with 600 people. My brother was concerned that those in Hindu society would be hostile towards me for taking on a role that is normally reserved for men. In fact, it was the opposite, and I had really good feedback. All the young ones ran up to me afterwards and said, 'We've never seen a woman priest.' I had so much positivity, and that was the start of becoming a Hindu priestess. Being a priestess has helped me with my own spiritual journey. I've moved away from the ritualistic Hinduism I grew up with and progressed to a more philosophical and experiential Hinduism.

My mother was a storyteller, as was her mother. When we were children and my father travelled all the time doing his priestly things, I remember we used to sit outside under the beautiful African sky full of stars as bright as lightbulbs. Sometimes children from the neighbourhood would join in and my mother would tell stories that she had heard from her mother. The stories were sometimes religious and other times they were fables and mythological tales, and often the protagonist of the tale was a strong woman.

Chandrika doing a Deepa Yaga ritual at the Sanatan Dharma Mandal and Hindu Community Centre, Cardiff

I started telling stories at the Cardiff storytelling circle about eight years ago. I recently won a mentorship programme with the Beyond the Border Storytelling Festival, which has allowed me to transition from a casual teller of tales to a professional storyteller. I am currently working with Arts Council Wales as a creative practitioner, exploring the concept of multicultural Wales with schoolchildren. With that project on the go, I am now retiring from dentistry.

I feel that whatever is right for you happens, as life is a journey and not a destination. The universe gives you what you need, even if it does not give you what you want. What does not break you, makes you, and the thing to do is keep an open heart and accept what comes your way as a blessing.

# Promises from the Heart

## Indu Deglurkar
**CONSULTANT CARDIOTHORACIC SURGEON**

*Everyone would say cardiothoracic surgery is a male-dominated field, but to me, it's a field that predominately consists of males. The fact that I'm female didn't hold me back from being competitive. However, gender and race discrimination have always existed both overtly and covertly. It's important to have the mental resilience and self-belief to pursue your dream and succeed.*

I was born in Arakonam, in the state of Tamil Nadu in India. My father was the deputy chief personnel officer in the South Central Railways, and my mum was a housewife, devoting all her time to our upbringing. I'm the youngest of five girls. We were quite boisterous and had a lot of fun playing with all the kids around and being competitive in everything we did. I remember all the love and affection from my family, and being the youngest, I was quite spoiled but totally nurtured and cared for.

At the age of seven, I'd made up my mind that I was going to be a heart surgeon. I remember seeing pictures of heart-lung machines and cardiac surgeons in magazines and telling my dad this was what I want to do and asking him what I needed to study to become a cardiac surgeon. At school, I sketched a scene of an operating theatre with me on the right side, wearing dangling earrings. I kept that picture on my wall for years, adding my degrees next to it.

Indu in medical school, 1987

My desire never wavered all through school. Getting into medical school in India is extremely difficult and competitive. Only on one occasion, I mentioned to my dad that if I failed to get into medical school, I would join the foreign service, but it didn't come to that. I also wanted to obtain a Fellowship of the Royal Colleges of Surgeons (FRCS) and train as a surgeon in the UK. I landed during peak winter in December and couldn't bear the cold climate. I arrived alone, as my husband, Mukund, was finishing his Master's in trauma and orthopaedics. My sister-in-law helped me prepare for the PLAB exam, which is for overseas doctors. I did the exam within three weeks of arriving, and I failed in the attempt.

Tragedy struck the family when both of Mukund's grandparents died on the same day. A few weeks later, my father-in-law had a massive myocardial infarction and also passed away. I had married into a very famous, traditional, conservative Marathi family, where women were housewives, and no woman had ever immigrated to another country. My father-in-law was highly supportive and encouraged me to chase my dreams. His last words to me on the night he passed away were that he wanted to see me persevere and succeed. Equally so, my

Indu and her husband, Mukund receiving their FRCS qualifications from the Royal College of Surgeons, 1997

parents have always wanted me to succeed and become a consultant cardiac surgeon. They supported my dreams, and my desire to fulfil my promise to them became a huge driving force to succeed, despite all the hardships.

The next available slot to do the PLAB exam was in six months' time. I was living as a paying guest, and finance became a major hurdle. My family were happy to fund me, but I didn't want to burden them. My husband's friend from medical school was working in Wales and helped me to obtain a clinical attachment in orthopaedics at Morriston Hospital. For months until my exam, I had a room at the hospital and very little money. The change in my

Indu's parents (*middle row, first and second on the left*) and her family, 1995

circumstances and lifestyle was dramatically different from what it was at home. I made a lot of friends very quickly, but I didn't seek any help from anyone until I'd passed the exam.

I was grief-stricken with losing three members of my family and being so far away from home made it very difficult. I would do ward rounds and theatres and study in the evenings for the exam. Failure, as well as financial and emotional adversity, test your resilience and change you for the better. My friends who helped me through the journey are with me even now. I flew back home to India after passing the exam and put my head on my mum's lap, and sobbed endlessly. It was the first time anyone at home had any indication of the challenges I had faced.

When I started training in cardiac surgery, female doctors were automatically typecast into certain roles. Colleagues assumed that I was an anaesthetist rather than a cardiac surgeon. I had to constantly battle with racial and gender bias to pursue my passion for cardiac surgery. However, my work, capability and dedication earned the respect of my colleagues.

There were no female role models and very few female surgeons. My trainers were male surgeons who've had unwavering confidence in my ability, and there are skill sets I've learned from different people, including my junior staff. Being ethnic and female in a foreign country is a triple challenge and a potentially insurmountable barrier. In recognition of this, the European Association of Cardiothoracic Surgeons invited me to give a talk to all the aspiring female cardiac surgeons. Nowadays, you can offer mentorship to people who want to train as cardiac surgeons, but such a privilege was rare in the past.

There were big challenges throughout the training programme, due to very long working hours, poor work-life balance and being pregnant in a setting where the shortest operation would be three and a half hours. Despite a difficult pregnancy, I carried on operating and running around dealing with cardiac arrests. It challenged my mental and physical resilience, and it really was a case of mind over matter.

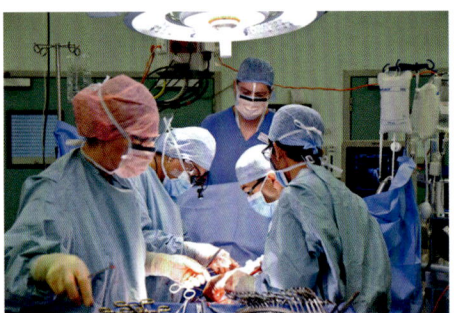

Indu and medical team performing the first ever total hybrid aortic arch replacement in Wales, 2016

I probably would have had a few more children if the work-life balance had been more congenial. We did not have European working time directives, and we started at 6.30am and went home late at night. Weekends on call were tough, and whenever I was an on-call resident away from home, Mukund, who's also a surgeon, would bring our son, Abhishek, to the workplace so that he could see his mum. It was a big challenge, but it worked out, as Mukund helped in every possible way.

I've been working for many years as a consultant cardiothoracic surgeon at the University Hospital of Wales in Cardiff. I perform highly complex operations, specialise in aortic surgery, high-risk surgery in the elderly, offer a service for patients with special needs and operate on people that have been turned down or have come from abroad. Surgery is very complex and labour intensive, and twelve to fourteen-hour operations are quite routine. It's an extreme end involving technical and non-technical skills, which are intricate, challenging and require physical and mental resilience.

Until 2013, there were only five female heart surgeons in the UK. Most people believe cardiothoracic surgery is a male-dominated field, but to me, it is just a field consisting predominantly of males. The fact that I'm female didn't hold me back from being competitive, though gender and race discrimination have always existed, both overtly and covertly.

I feel quite strongly that doctors should play a greater part in running the National Health Service and take on executive roles. I founded the Welsh Cardiothoracic Society, led my department for more than six years and represented 695 Consultants as the chair of the Senior Medical Staff Committee for seven years. I have done an Emerging Leaders Fellowship at the Royal College, a Postgraduate Medical Leadership course, and won a fellowship to attend an international leadership course at Harvard University. I was awarded the Welsh Asian Women's Science, Medicine and Technology award several years ago and was shortlisted for the UK Asian Women of Achievement National Award.

Our lives have revolved around our son, but there have been difficult moments when you want to be home for important events but could not because of an emergency. The most beautiful part is that our son always understood that there is a certain responsibility attached to our jobs, and he's very proud of the fact that his mum is a surgeon.

Indu, Mukund and their son, Abhishek, as head boy at Cathedral School, Llandaff, 2019

Despite the long working hours, whatever time we spent together as a family was high-quality time. Abhishek is a bright, confident child, who's done well in school, and is now doing his A levels. My ability to contribute at a high level at work stems from the support of my family and friends. The most beautiful moments in our lives are family orientated.

My roots are still in India, and my mum, two sisters and my in-laws reside in Hyderabad. India is an intricate part of our lives, and Mukund, Abhishek and I visit there frequently. I also visit India for professional reasons, as an invited chair for international conferences or to give talks on aortic surgery, which is my speciality interest. It is a great opportunity to guide aspiring surgeons to the UK, including women.

Mukund's family, with Mukund in the back row next to Indu, who is standing in front of her mother-in-law, while there is a photo of her late father-in-law on the wall, 2013

We have helped a number of people who stay with us while preparing for their exams in the UK, so they don't go through the same kind of trauma that I did. It's satisfying to give that extra support and reinforcing that they are capable of succeeding. Nothing worthwhile is ever easy to achieve. The more challenging it is, the more you'll enjoy the success.

I would say to a young woman starting out that if you have the ability to do it, you have to pursue your dream. You mustn't waver, even when there is adversity. Difficult paths are never going to be smooth. It's important to have the confidence and the mental resilience to pursue your dream. It's also important to have the support of your family, friends and colleagues because nobody achieves anything on their own. I think the people around you are vital for your mental health and happiness, and when you are going through difficult times, support from family and friends is very crucial.

Several years ago, my mum and nephew came to a talk I delivered in Bangalore. The chairman announced that my mum was in the audience, and she received an ovation like I've never heard before. As she sat listening to my talk about complex aortic surgery, she had tears streaming down her cheeks because I think it was at that point that her dreams for me were realised after a long time. It was a very precious feeling, and even looking back on it now, several years later, I still have warmth in my heart when I think that my family is feeling very proud of me right now.

# Healthy Living

## Kamila Hawthorne
**GENERAL PRACTITIONER, MEDDYGFA GLAN CYNON SURGERY, MOUNTAIN ASH**
**HEAD OF GRADUATE ENTRY MEDICINE, SWANSEA UNIVERSITY**

*Some mountains seem very high to climb; it's just taking one step at a time, and you'll get there, which is what happened with me. I still worry about what the future holds and whether I'll get to where I want to go. I think that's the human condition, but if you have confidence, you'll be alright.*

I was born in Edinburgh, Scotland, where my parents, who were very young doctors, were completing their post-graduate training in medicine. Both my parents are of Indian origin, but my father was born and grew up in Tanganyika (which became Tanzania). When I was six months old, he decided to go back home to Tanganyika because he couldn't find a job in the UK, so we turned up in Dar es Salaam in late 1960. So my first language was Swahili, and my memories of being a child and having fun are all based in Africa. I remember being very hot, and it was extremely unusual to wear anything other than a very thin cotton dress and sandals. I remember playing outdoors, climbing trees, swinging, going to the beach, and feeling perfectly safe.

My father worked as a paediatrician for the government, earning peanuts. My mother had wanted to do obstetrics and gynaecology, but ended up working in general practice in order to earn enough money to keep the family going. By the time we left Tanzania in 1970, my mum had a very thriving practice, just seeing women and children, and my father set up paediatric services across the country, becoming known nationally and internationally. When the situation became more restrictive for Asian

Kamila, age 4 with her father in Dar es Salaam

people, and we were seeking to leave Tanzania, my father was offered a job in London at Great Ormond Street in the Tropical Child Health Unit, so he came first and a few months later, we followed.

You grow up pretty fast when you come to the UK from another country. I went to an inner-city primary state school in Putney, which was quite racist and tough, and very different from the private school for international students I'd left in Dar es Salaam. But as a child, you just get on with it. After a term, my parents sent me to a girls' private school in Sydenham, but in a funny way, it was worse than the state school because I was the first non-white child in the school, and that was even tougher, actually.

Having said that, I got a good education and went on to do my medical degree at Oxford. During the six years I was there, I met my husband, Barney, who was also a medical student, and we married shortly after I qualified. My husband is English, and people have asked me how I broke away from my background and culture, and the truth is that I didn't—my parents did. My father is from a Muslim family and my mother from a Hindu family, so they were the ones who broke away. And they've always been very happy with my husband, who's a sweetie, so it's never been a real problem for us, and we've been very lucky.

After I qualified as a doctor in 1984, my initial jobs were in Oxford, Reading and Nottingham. Around that time, in 1990, I developed an interest in diabetes and discovered that while Type 2 diabetes was much more common in people of Asian origin, a significant number of Asians with the condition knew almost nothing about how to treat it.

I had an idea, based on something I'd seen when I was a medical student, of using pictorial flashcards to provide health education. It seemed like a great idea for South Asian patients who spoke little English, while many of the women could not read in any language. We did some trials in Manchester, where I was living at the time, having link workers, who could speak the same language, use the flashcards with Asian people in their homes or community settings, and found that afterwards, especially with the women, there was a significant improvement in their diabetic control. It was very interesting to reach out and connect with people, who at first, seemed very different to me, and I loved getting to know them.

I was able to use the flashcards again when we moved to Cardiff in 1995. A GP in the Riverside area of Cardiff contacted me asking for help with her Bangladeshi patients, many of whom were developing diabetes early on

Kamila being presented with a Doctor of the Year Award by the president of the British Polio Society, c.2010

or having strokes or heart attacks and dying young. I thought I should be turning my research into service. It took us ages to get funding, but in the end, we got some money from the Bro Taf Health Authority and rolled out the flashcard programme to a number of GP practices and wrote a couple of research papers along the way.

In the early 2000s, I gathered together a healthcare team, and we were able to get a Welsh Assembly Government Health Innovation grant to set up the Heartlink Project, working with ethnic minority patients in thirteen practices in Cardiff. The aim of the project was to raise awareness of diabetes and heart disease among GP practices and patients. One thing we would do was to contact community or religious leaders and speak to their caterers regarding an upcoming festival to see if they could cook something that was culturally appropriate, while low in fat and sugar and high in fibre. Then we could talk to the people attending the event about healthier ways of cooking and keeping healthy, as well as the early signs of diabetes or heart disease.

We were also training GP practices in diabetes management, as well as race equality training, combining practices so they could discuss their shared knowledge of patients with each other. We ran a free, accredited distance learning course in diabetes management, so participants could get a certificate, which many did, seeing the value of it. That project lasted about five years and was very exciting and enjoyable. It was also perhaps a precursor, fifteen years before its time, to the GP clusters that exist in Wales today.

Around that time, my career took a bit of a turn because

Kamila in her inaugural lecture as president of the Cardiff Medical Society, 2011

I became more involved in the Royal College of GPs. I'd been an examiner for their membership exam for a long time, and in 2007, the college was given permission to convert their voluntary membership exam into the main licencing exam for general practice in Britain, so it suddenly became a very high-stakes exam that you had to take if you wanted to be a GP. I was involved in developing that exam, which now included a clinical component. It was a great honour, and I thoroughly enjoyed working with like-minded GPs from all over the UK. In 2015, I became vice-chair of the college for the next three years, covering their professional development on a national level.

These experiences, to some extent, set the rest of my career because I switched from patient health education to the education of medical students and trainee doctors. In 2010, I was asked to redevelop the undergraduate curriculum for medical students in Cardiff to make it more modern and community-facing, so I incorporated things I'd learned as a GP and through projects like Heartlink, like having a close clinical relationship with patients earlier on and maintaining a strong community focus. The new curriculum was introduced in Cardiff in 2012 and has been a great success. It's also been really rewarding to talk about general practice as a career to medical students and to try and pass on some of the enthusiasm that other people had given me in the past.

Some of the challenges I've faced have been the frequent moves in my early career because I was following my husband's career moves, so it was difficult to get some coherency in my own career. Also, balancing a career with motherhood is never comfortable. You try to be there for your children and put them first, but you don't always manage, particularly if you've got commitments that clash with what your child needs. My husband and I looked after the children together, and I'm very lucky to have earned enough to afford a daytime nanny, but it would have been lovely to have had family nearby. My kids are grown up now—my older one, Rehana, is a GP trainee and my younger one, Tim, is a junior doctor, so it must run in the family!

I'm now in Mountain Ash, working as a GP in a completely different practice, which has been quite exciting. It's a very established community, and there are no people of colour there, apart from me. It's also very deprived, and we're looking at ways of reducing social isolation and of helping people with moderate mental health problems, other than through prescribing pills. For example, we've made links with a community garden, to which we can refer patients, and we're also a Parkrun practice, so we're pushing physical activity as being healthy and improving wellbeing. It's great having these challenges and developing new ways to help people and improve what we do.

Kamila with her husband, Barney, receiving an MBE, 2016

I've also taken up a role as the head of Graduate Entry Medicine at Swansea University, running the four-year programme and training medical students. While it's quite a responsibility, I have lots of ideas to bring their curriculum up to date and to introduce a really community-facing aspect to the programme. My years of experience in community work and general practice are being fed into this new role, and it's interesting how different aspects of my work overlap and build on each other.

I would say to people to dare to dream and don't feel that you can't do something because you probably can. And while some mountains seem very high to climb, if you just take one step at a time, you'll get there, which is what happened with me. I still worry about what the future holds and whether I'll get to where I want to go. I think that's the human condition. So what I would say to the younger me is to have confidence and you'll be alright.

# Pioneering Public Health Genomics

## Layla Jader
**DOCTOR SPECIALISING IN PUBLIC HEALTH AND GENOMICS**

*When you know it's good to push in a certain direction, you have to believe in yourself in order to achieve. And if you are coming from somewhere else and want to succeed, you have to put in more effort and hard work to be part of the system. You also need to have more patience and stamina, not to give up when you face obstacles that are inevitable.*

I grew up in Baghdad, which, although it had a lot of political troubles, was developing and improving exponentially in health, education and literacy. I was one of six girls and had a lovely childhood and, as you would imagine in a house full of girls, it was a lot of fun. My parents were both educationalists. My mother was a primary school teacher and my father was a reader in mathematics at Baghdad University.

We had a good, professional home environment. Our father put us in a private school run by French nuns, the Dominican Sisters of the Presentation. I don't know how he managed to put four of us in that costly school, but he wanted to make sure we learned languages and achieved our full potential and obtained good careers. My eleven years of school were the best of my life, and I achieved very high records throughout. With my father's encouragement, the need to achieve has influenced me for the rest of my life. This can be a bit of a curse because it might be stressful, as you want to be at the top and achieve to the best of your ability. However, I would not change my life because it made me who I am, and I have always made the best of what opportunities I got.

I then went to medical school in Baghdad, a six-year degree course. My oldest sister was in medicine and the second one in pharmacy, so it was almost inevitable that I followed. It was at university that I met my husband who was in my year. We fell in love and got married in the final year. Our daughter was born a year later while I was on rotation in different hospitals. It was very difficult, but we had our extended family who supported us, which helped a great deal. I started training in anaesthetics, which was not actually my first choice, but it was an opportunity to stay in Baghdad and to have family support for my little child.

Then an opportunity arose for me to study for a diploma in London, which is how we came to Britain in 1978 when my daughter was two and a half years old. After a year in London, I got a post in anaesthetics at Singleton Hospital, Swansea, and took a diploma in anaesthetics. Four years later, we had another baby. With one parent in anaesthesia and another in paediatrics, and with both having on calls, it was just impossible with two young children. There was no family support whatsoever, so the first few years were a real struggle.

As such, I decided to change my speciality from anaesthesia to genetics, which I fell in love with. The atmosphere at the Institute of Medical Genetics was like a beehive full of high achievers, and I worked and conducted research, culminating in an MD thesis. I will never forget the positive influence that my supervisor, the late professor, Sir Peter Harper, had on my career. I wanted to emulate the academic atmosphere around me, and although my contract was part-time, I immersed myself working full time because that's what I loved to do.

I stayed there for five years, published several papers, and presented at international conferences, packing a lot into those years. I wanted to continue specialising in genetics, but my background was anaesthesia, so I decided to go into public health training with the idea that I would maintain my interest and close connection with genetics through the lens of public health. I reviewed advances in genetics and analysed their impact on public health policies, proposing a change to those policies based on new genomic knowledge.

In 1999, I was appointed as consultant/senior clinical lecturer in public health genomics, the first in the country. There is now a small community of public health genomic specialists in the UK, but I was one of those early pioneers who established this subspecialty. When I was a senior registrar in public health medicine, I carried out research on antenatal screening. The system was fragmented, and women were ill-informed about screening. As such, I decided to set up a multidisciplinary group to develop a screening programme for the Bro Taf Health Authority. As part of my research, I interviewed women through their antenatal screening, including those who ended up having affected babies.

It was pioneering to be able to use the words of those women to effect change, and I published several papers on this project, including a chapter in the *Nature Encyclopedia of the Human Genome*. With my team, I launched a pioneering programme covering all aspects of antenatal screening, including creating the role of screening midwife, plus producing booklets and educational courses for midwives and obstetricians, as well as a database, audit and an annual review. This made a big impact nationally and became a model for several regions throughout the UK. In 1999, I was a finalist for Hospital Doctor of the Year, and as a group, we won The Golden Helix UK and

Layla presenting at a symposium she organised at Public Health Wales, 2014

Pan-European Awards. I am immensely proud of these achievements.

Following a public health reorganisation in Wales, I worked for a short period as a director of public health. This was the first time I wrote about my vision of how to improve inequalities in health, which is through prioritising and improving the health and education of children from the time of conception, throughout pregnancy, and up until they finish school.

Later, studying epigenetics, which is the impact of the environment on the genomes, my review highlighted a critical period around puberty, in which environmental factors influence the genomes that will form future generations. As such, it is very crucial that we prioritise children's health until they are eighteen, as well as their education, which also affects health. I started campaigning in the last ten years, and I aim to continue by raising awareness at every opportunity.

Working with the genetic community, I did not feel any discrimination. Three-quarters of the staff were women, and many were of foreign backgrounds, and everyone was valued for the quality of their work. The first time I felt differently, sadly, was later when I was working in other places. Not only I was a woman and from a foreign background, but I was also highly qualified professionally, coming up with solutions to alleviate inequalities in health. Although my advice was taken and money was invested accordingly, there were some who made sure that I had a difficult and stressful time and I felt blocked at every turn. I was told that the country could not afford to prioritise beyond a child's first 1,000 days, though I argued that science has shown us that we need to prioritise all children or risk the implications for future generations.

I set up symposia and courses to inform everyone, most of which are still on the internet. Sadly, those who put obstacles did not turn up to learn, some of them being in managerial roles, so it was like a wall. They must have felt threatened by a capable woman who was not only working extremely hard but was obviously doing good quality work, so they put obstacles in my way, which was painful.

Working in NHS Wales for 37 years, I met people of the highest calibre who supported my career, and I will always be indebted to them. Most of the British are fair-minded people once they come to know you, but if you are coming from somewhere else, you must put in more effort, patience, and hard work if you want to succeed. I managed to achieve quite a lot, which is a testament to my perseverance. Being proudly awarded a Lifetime Achievement Award in 2017, which was judged by a national panel of senior academics, was a good testament of fairness and a final affirmation of the quality of work I have managed to achieve.

When you know it's good to push in a certain direction, you have to believe in yourself in order to achieve, so my advice for young women starting out is that you must have stamina and not to give up when you face obstacles which are inevitable. If you have a social network to rely on and seek support, it will be an easier journey to achieve what you aim and hope for.

To my pleasure, my daughters followed me into medicine,

Layla winning the Lifetime Achievement Award, 2017

so I must have done something right. They saw the excitement on my face when I achieved, and they also saw me down when there were obstacles in my way, and they learned from it. Both are doing so well, and I am very proud of them. They are both married to local doctors, and I have four wonderful grandchildren, for whom I am eternally grateful. We are a close-knit family, very much part of the community, and we are now heavily involved in local charity work. We love Wales, and it has been our home for over 40 years. There were opportunities for us to work abroad, but we felt passionate about Wales and did not ever want to move away.

Layla with her husband and two daughters in Cardiff, 2017

# The Way to the Future

## Loren Henry
**CO-FOUNDER OF URBAN CIRCLE AND G-EXPRESSIONS**

*Growing up, my mum made me understand that no matter what happens in your life, you can learn from it, which then turns it into a positive because, at the end of the day, it can show you how you want to be.*

Loren (*right*), age 10, with mum holding brother, Ladell; and brother, Romell; and sister, Venisa

I was born in Newport and have one sister and two brothers. My father left when I was three, and I can still remember the day that he went. My dad's presence wasn't about from then on, but my mum's always raised me to have respect for my father regardless, and to make up my own mind about him and to have a relationship with him on my own terms.

Between keeping the house and raising four kids, my mum worked every day of her life, mainly holding down cleaning jobs. She was also in direct sales and ended up working her way up to be a regional manager, so she earned good money along the way. As a working woman, my mum was out most of the time, but my brother and sister were awesome in looking after me. When I got of age, I did the cooking myself and made sure we had food on the table before my mum came back from work.

I was very active in primary school and played football and hockey. I was also very creative and imaginative and was always dancing and singing, even though I couldn't sing a note. But I was good at organising things and getting people together to showcase their talent. At the age of fourteen, I found out about a place called the DEN, which was a council-led project that worked with young people aged fourteen to eighteen, giving them advice about safe sex, drugs and alcohol. This was my first experience of having a place to go where me and my friends could hang out and do all the things we liked doing in an environment with adults – other than family members – who took the time to listen to what we really wanted and began to support and facilitate our creative nature and individual talents.

By the age of sixteen, I helped to create a group called True Life, which was a team of young people spreading the message through songs we had created about the importance of safe sex and how drugs and alcohol are not cool. We had many experiences, from residentials to organising and planning showcases, but more importantly, we got to perform on stage while spreading a positive message. Unfortunately, this all came to an abrupt end as funding ran out, which meant that our new family members could no longer be paid for the time they spent with us, and the building we called our own was taken away. That was the day I decided I would run my own organisation based on the arts for young people – but also run by young people – and, little did I know, that this would be the beginning of the journey.

I loved to travel, to be adventurous and to find my own feet. My mum supported me as long as I got my work done or had money to pay for things. She facilitated my interests and instilled independence in me from an early age, so by the time I was fourteen, I was quite streetwise and out all the time. I also had my first job at weekends at Megabowl, which I was good at, so I earned a lot through tips and got a taste for earning my own money, which enabled me to do what I wanted. When I was sixteen, I went with my sister

Loren with members of Project U-Turn, featuring teenage boys from various backgrounds celebrating diversity through sport and music, while also offering meaningful and accredited learning opportunities

and female cousins on an amazing trip to Ayia Napa, a party island in Cyprus. I had the best time, and it was the start of my journey learning about DJs, promotion, bookings and making the right contacts to be able to set myself up in events.

In 2006, I set up an organisation for young people called Urban Circle Productions and got National Lottery funding to pay for a building, plus an administrator and myself as a part-time project coordinator. We were open from seven in the morning till eleven at night. Young people used to access us before they went to school and after school as well, and the ones that didn't really have anywhere to go would stay until our doors closed. Two years later, we had 1,000 young people on our books and we were doing four massive events throughout the year.

Urban Circle was a place where the young people were

Loren with members of the Urban Circle Youth Management team at the Urban Circle Summer Fest, 2019

able to be themselves. Everyone has different starts in life, and a lot of the young people I've worked with have come from poverty or broken homes, so they're already at a disadvantage. The only thing we can really do is to provide a safe space and to try and give young people the tools or the education to help them change their negative thought processes and give them a better start for themselves. It was also giving them a care element that's been absent from their lives. They haven't been as blessed as me to have someone who cares for me as much as my mum does. So that's what I put into my work, and I think that's what has enabled the organisation to blossom the way it has. I also thoroughly enjoy what I do.

In 2010, a law was passed requiring someone from the organisation to be degree educated. None of us was, and we didn't want to hire someone who might have wanted to take Urban Circle in a different direction. However, I had no intention of going to university because I'm dyslexic. But we drew straws, and I drew the short straw. Initially, I was not happy, but it turned out to be the best day of my life. I was always trying to take young people out of their comfort zones and get them to educate themselves to be able to do what they needed to do. So they gave me the courage and strength to pursue what I needed to do to be able to facilitate them further.

I did a youth and community work degree. The first year of the course was incredibly hard, but I had a lot of support. The theory, policy and modules were all things I'd been doing in my work, so I enjoyed it because I could identify ways I could facilitate my organisation better and put them into practice. Then my tutors put me forward with a scholarship to do a Master's degree, which was Working with Children and Young People. I was reluctant at first, but as it was paid, I thought, I couldn't say no to that opportunity.

The Master's degree taught me more about policy and government and made me realise that the organisation I'd set up is actually doing what statutory organisations say that they would like to do, but instead of being tokenistic, Urban Circle actually listens to young people and lets them lead. We've been going for fifteen years now, and many of the young people that came through are some of the main workers now. In 2010, we ended up having to set up a sub-organisation, G-Expressions, which focuses more on the dance side of things, purely out of how many young people who came through the doors who wanted to dance. I worked with my younger cousin because she was so passionate about it and so good at dancing, while I had to put myself on a dance course to make sure I was doing things safely with the youth.

G-Expressions has grown quite quickly through Arts Council and High Sheriff funding. I've had six young people

Loren at her BA Honours graduation, with mother, Deanna and older brother, Romell, 2011

Loren presenting participants of a G-Expressions Level 2 Dance Leaders Course with their qualifications, 2020

come through and do their degrees, and they're now qualified youth workers working between both G-Expressions and Urban Circle. We've also now set up an educational arm in G-Expressions, delivering Dance Leader qualifications Levels 1, 2 and 3, and have over 300 young people who've gained these qualifications.

We're now looking at getting a purpose-built building, so I'm working on getting the core funding to come through for this. I'm also trying to get the organisations to a point where they're self-sufficient, as you can only give so much of yourself and you can't run on empty. I recently took some time off to travel for a year. I went to China for nine months and learnt Tai Chi, Shaolin Kung Fu and Wing Chun. The experience was amazing, and I loved it. I'm currently studying agriculture because I want to learn plant pathology, and I want to go to South Africa for two years to do my Master's. Once I get that, I'm going to go home to Antigua/Jamaica to grow my own food and just chill – that's all I want to do.

I would say to anyone starting out that it's important to get the right qualifications and to put yourself through the paces of experiences and hands-on work. Never lose faith in your goals, and just keep building your self-confidence because what you want can definitely materialise, especially if you're passionate and have the drive. Then all you need are the tools to educate yourself in those fields and to have fun with it and enjoy. It can be hard, but just keep at it and ask for help if you need it to do what you want to do well.

My mum has been the main role model in my life. She's my rock and has shown me basically everything. Growing up, my mum made me understand that no matter what happens in your life, you can learn from it, which then turns it into a positive because, at the end of the day, it can show you how you want to be.

# Landing on her Feet

## Kiran Ratna
**BHARATANATYAM DANCER AND TEACHER, FOUNDER OF INDIA DANCE WALES (NOW INDIA DANCE BN)**

*Dance solidifies a lot of things, like identity to be proud of. It also breaks many barriers.*

I was born in Kenya, and when I was three months old, we moved to India. My parents were both British-born, and my father decided to come to England when I was a year old, while I stayed in the Punjab, in India, with my mother, siblings and grandparents. When I was twelve, my mother moved to England, and I came a few months later. I was the youngest and the only one under eighteen, so I could come as a dependent, but my siblings had to wait two years for their visas.

I was very excited to be going to England to live with both my parents for the first time. I arrived one April, and my father picked me up from the airport. On the train journey to Birmingham, I remember all was grey, miserable and boring, and all the houses looked like huts! It was also very cramped at the house we arrived in, but I was very happy.

In India, I was everyone's favourite and did well in school, but here I was looked down upon for coming from a 'backward country'. It didn't bother me very much, as I

Family photo, with Kiran standing in the middle, age 8

thought, what do they know? I, also, think because I felt I belonged to India and it was okay to be treated a bit differently. I believe that it was lucky for me, really, to have had that confidence in my self-identity.

My father was very adamant that I should go to a grammar school. Though I had missed the eleven-plus entrance exam for grammar school, he took me to the local girls' grammar school and asked the headteacher to test me. I did way above average in mathematics but below average in English. However, the headteacher decided to take me on anyway. There weren't many Indian girls at the school. Eventually, my best friend became an Irish girl called Mandy, who had very long blonde hair, while I had long black hair. We both shared and learnt a lot from each other, but she moved back to Ireland a year later.

In Punjab, many relatives would come and visit us, and the house was always full of people. In England, it was just me and my parents in a rented accommodation. As they were both working, I spent a lot of time alone and remember being uncomfortable and often scared. My father was very keen for me to adapt and learn things, so he enrolled me into the library and taught me how to catch buses and practical things, and I adjusted quite quickly.

I could sense my mother was missing her other children a lot, so I was regularly praying that they would come soon. Two years later, they came. The day that they came was quite momentous. We borrowed someone's van and drove to Heathrow. Without having a phone, we instead received a telegram saying the flight was delayed by a day, so we had to stay the night with a relative near Heathrow.

From then, my life changed a lot. Although they were a lot older than me, I had to teach my siblings about life in the UK. There was a big generation gap, and I'd had my most impressionable years in a very different environment to them. The bond I thought I had with them had changed.

In our family, education was very important, and I was adamant that I was going to go to university and do

Kiran's university graduation photo, 1983

engineering. Fortunately, through university grants and being able to work in summer holidays, I was able to do so, which was good because it taught me to be independent and self-sufficient. In university, there were students from all over the world, so it didn't really matter if I was Indian or not. In fact, I was probably more English than some because I had gone to school here.

Amazingly, my parents were fine with me doing engineering, though my brothers were not – a girl doing engineering? And for an Indian girl to be moving away from home for the university was also quite a thing in those days. So going to university was probably the biggest thing of my life, as in living independently, financially and otherwise, but they were happy days.

In those days, being a female engineer was a big deal, especially an Indian female engineer, and with my name often misspelt as Kieran, I was frequently mistaken as a man in documents. My first job was with the Ministry of Defence, where my induction was to go around different departments. Engineering or research development was fine for a woman, but in departments like manufacturing, they weren't used to the idea of a female engineer, and on top of that, one that was not white. But I was happy in my own skin and accepted that I was different. I remember one of them asking me where I was from, and when I said India, he asked when I was going back and didn't I miss my family? I told him they were all here, and that was quite a shock for him. But that was in those days. I don't think it would happen now.

Parallel to that was my dance journey. In India, from a young age, I was learning *Kathak,* and I was good at it and loved it. Unfortunately, in my junior school in India, I broke my arm, and soon after that, I came to England. My dance teacher encouraged me to continue with my dance in the UK and said that he'd heard that people have opportunities like being on television. So when I came here, I was just doing *Kathak* to any classical-sounding music from wherever I could find and stitching my own costumes.

One time there was a talent competition in my school and I went as a dancer and everyone was very impressed. So dance gave me something to be proud of and kept me connected to India and my culture. In my teens, a Bharatanatyam dance teacher, Chitraleka Bolar, came from India to Birmingham, and I started learning with her. As a university student in Cardiff, I performed at a Diwali function, and I was asked to teach dance at the Rubicon Dance Centre. I didn't want to, as I was still learning, but later in 1982, I started teaching and also continued doing little performances. I was the first one to teach Bharatanatyam dance in Wales, educating the public and sharing the passion, which has been very satisfying.

I met my husband at university. I came from a traditional Punjabi family, and dance was not the thing for a girl to be doing, especially after marriage, but I was very adamant that I would only marry someone who would let me dance. So luckily for me, my husband is a Tamil from south India, and they're especially respectful towards Bharatanatyam.

Then I had my son and daughter and was still teaching, performing and working as an engineer. I had no family in Wales, and my husband had quite an intense job himself, so

being a mother was quite a big challenge, and it was a lot to manage. Eventually, I gave up my engineering career and took up dance full time, which was more workable with children. I formed the Kiran Ratna Company, which later became India Dance Wales and since renamed India Dance BN. Megan Lloyd heads the branch in Wales, while my daughter, Vibha Selvaratnam, who's also a research scientist, is propagating Bharatanatyam in a brand new area, Devon!

In the 1980s and 1990s, I used to work in schools quite a bit, so I would be dressed up as a Bharatanatyam dancer dropping the kids off at school. I think my children definitely saw the dance as enriching their lives, as opposed to, 'Oh my God, what's our mother doing?' It became part of their lives too and something that was fun and to be proud of. They both learnt it from childhood, and my daughter has taken it on seriously.

I remember when my son was fourteen, he accompanied me to a workshop for teachers in Newport, and when asked about his opinion on what I was doing, he said, 'I'm proud of my mum because she's proud of who she is, and she just does what she enjoys.' I think it's great for a fourteen-year-old to appreciate that, and I hope that he's as comfortable in his skin as I am.

When I became a teacher and a mother, I could see that in the younger generation, dance breaks

Kiran with husband, Dr Selvaratnam, and son, Dr Prashant Selvaratnam and daughter, Vibha Selvaratnam, 2017

through barriers, gives you an identity and enriches a lot of aspects. It's also an art form that isn't just for Indians. It's not something you're just born with, and just because you're born Hindu, you're not born a Bharatanatyam dancer. Everyone has to learn it, and I had non-Indians of all races and religious backgrounds as students. This also helped the Indians to see that other people appreciated the dance, so we should too, and that being Indian is not something to hide but something to be proud of.

Wales is a bit more clued in with cultural values, as they have their own language and so on, so they value people wanting to maintain their heritage a bit more. I grew up hearing the word 'tolerance,' which in my mind is a little negative. Instead of tolerating, we should accept and respect all people and be open and sharing together. I was lucky to be teaching at the Rubicon Dance Centre because

Kiran and daughter, Vibha, at a school performance in Cardiff, 1998

it exposed me to the whole community, not just the Indian populace. Things are much more global now, and Cardiff has changed a lot with a greater Indian population now, compared to the 1980s.

Circumstances dictate at times which way you go. I wasn't ever expecting to be having my own dance company. So you need to value what talents and qualities you have within you, and use them appropriately, and not kill yourself being what you're not. Be yourself, and at the same time, keep learning, keep your options and your mind open and don't narrow your opportunities or underestimate your abilities. You never know what life may throw at you, so be flexible, accept, adapt, trust yourself and go with the flow.

Kiran at a reception at Buckingham Palace to launch the UK–India Year of Culture, 2017

# The Call of Music

## Dr Sarita Pawar BSc, MBBS, FRCOG, MRCGP, Diploma in GUM, Dermatology, Diabetes
**GP DOCTOR, CARDIFF**

*If you want to achieve your dreams, you need to stay positive, even in adversity, and be resilient with self-belief.*

I was born in Dehradun, India, the youngest of three daughters, followed by a son. Looking back, growing up in India was a fantastic time. I had a very privileged childhood and upbringing with no worries or restrictions and was allowed to dream, which set the foundations for my optimism, trust and hard work.

My father was a fighter pilot in the Indian Air Force and was an unorthodox and modern thinker who believed in educating his daughters and preparing them for any future hardships or struggles in life.

Sarita's father, Wing Commander Jagdish Bankapur, a fighter pilot with the Indian Air Force

My mother was a housewife, and due to ill-health, spent a lot of time in and out of hospital during the first eighteen months of my life. As such, I grew up more attached to my father and was 'daddy's girl', a very spoilt but much-loved child.

'Daddy's girl' Sarita (*seated on the right*) age 8, pictured with her siblings

My singing abilities were first noticed at the tender age of eight when my father heard me singing in the bathroom and announced to the family that I was going to be a singer one day. He lovingly called me his 'girl with the golden voice.' He always made me sing when we had parties and was very proud of me.

My first stage performance was a few years later when I sang a very popular song, 'Naina Barse' from the golden era of Bollywood films, and I received a standing ovation. My father tried to get me musical training, but I wasn't interested then, as I'd decided instead that I would be a doctor one day. Unlike most parents in India, my father wanted me to pursue a career in music but never forced me. Instead, he supported my childhood dreams to study and become a doctor.

I received an English-language education at a convent school and completed my schooling at the Air Force Central School in Delhi. As I needed an uninterrupted university education to pursue my chosen career, I left home to board when I was seventeen and moved to Pune, where I completed my BSc Honours degree in zoology with distinction. I went on to study for the MBBS medical degree at B. J. Medical College in Pune and qualified as a doctor.

Shortly thereafter, I got married and moved to Wales. I passed the Professional and Linguistic exam and commenced my medical career in the NHS in 1984. My first surgical job took me to King's Lynn, and after working in Liverpool and Southport, I returned to Wales. I had no difficulty adapting to life in the UK since my primary education had been in English, and there were many Indian doctors in the British hospitals.

The first ten years of my career were spent in secondary care, specialising in obstetrics and gynaecology. I decided to make a career change into primary care and general practice when my son was aged five, as I wanted to spend time with him during his formative years. I've never regretted this move, as it enabled me to have the perfect family and career balance.

From *Sarita Sings Thumri 2Day* album cover

While I was caught up with my career and family, my music took a back seat. However, I sang lullabies to my son, and when he was growing up, and I taxied him to school and after-school activities, I used the time in the car park to study for my membership and diploma exams and sang to myself to relax and reflect.

My brother, who had been my singing partner in India, had moved to America and became a singing sensation in Chicago. Inspired by his success, in the year 2000, I recorded my first album, *Khwaish* (A Desire), a collection of old and new Bollywood songs. I was invited to sing at the India Centre in Cardiff and subsequently joined the executive board as an active member.

The period which followed at the India Centre was full of music and dance, and was the most exciting time in my life in the UK. In 2010, I went on to record a further two albums with Pandit Vishwa Prakash, a Bollywood maestro from London who I'd met at the India Centre during one of his performances. These two albums, *Sarita Sings Thumri 2Day* and *Sarita Sings Tarana 2Day* were released at the Nehru Centre in London, and the launch was attended by the Indian Padma Bhushan maestro brothers, Rajan and Sajan Mishra and Mrs Raj Singhal as the chief guests. The event was also attended by my dear family and friends from Cardiff.

In 2011, I was awarded a prestigious WAWWA award in the Self Development category for my contributions to medicine and music. It was a proud moment for me, and the award helped give me the strength and resilience to overcome what followed next.

Sarita at her FRCOG ceremony, 2017

In 2015, I was a victim of hatred and malicious behaviour at my workplace, where I had been for over sixteen years. I was disappointed at the lack of support I received to help me fight for my principles. Rather than waste precious time or go into a state of depression, I decided, as I was advised, to swallow my misfortunes as a bitter pill, and moved on to rebuild my medical career in my twilight years, supported by my family and professional colleagues. This was, once again, a decision I did not regret. In 2016, I was awarded the Bharat Gaurav (Jewel of India), followed by a FRCOG in 2017, a BAPIO GP of the Year Award in 2018, and most recently, the MRCGP in 2021.

I am currently practising as a freelance general practitioner in Cardiff and have finally started training in Classical Indian vocal and instrumental music, having taken some time out from medicine for myself and my music. Life for me has been a journey along these two rails of medicine and music, and what a wonderful journey this combination has been. I truly feel so blessed.

If you want to achieve your dreams, you need to stay positive, even in adversity, and be resilient with self-belief. Parents and teachers lay the foundations, but you have to choose and work for the goals that you set for yourself.

# Inspiring others

# Soulful Resonance

## Patti Flynn
**SINGER, PERFORMER, PRESENTER, AUTHOR AND LOCAL HISTORIAN**

**In Tribute**

Patti was born in 1937 to a mixed-heritage family in Cardiff's docklands area, Tiger Bay. Patti's mum, Beatrice Maud, who was from Canton, Cardiff, worked in service for a Spanish family. They ran a very popular Cardiff restaurant on George Street, where many of the seamen enjoyed their meals when their ships docked for a few days to unload and load their cargo in the Cardiff port. It was here that Beatrice met Patti's father, Wilmott George, who was a merchant seaman from the coastal town of Saint Moria in the north of Jamaica.

The couple married and settled in the multiracial community of Tiger Bay, living in a shared house on Sophia Street. They had six children, three boys and three girls, with Patti being the youngest. When Patti was a year old, the family moved to their own three-bedroom house on Pomeroy Street, which had been given to them by Patti's uncle, Albert. Patti's mother later told her that she thought her dreams had been fulfilled when they were given the key to their own house.

Unfortunately, only a year after settling in, the Second World War began, and her mother's dreams began to shatter, with the family experiencing many war-related tragedies. Patti's father joined the Merchant Seamen, and his ship, while bringing much-needed resources to the UK, was torpedoed in September 1942. Then, two years later, Patti's older brother, Arthur, a sergeant in the Royal Air Force, was flying as a wireless operator-air gunner and was killed when his Lancaster

Patti with her cousin, Ronnie

bomber crashed in Lancashire. Arthur was 21 and had only just gained his wings that very same week.

Further sorrow soon befell the family. Patti's brother, Jocelyn, had signed on to work on a Japanese cargo ship trading at Cardiff docks. Months later, after the Japanese had bombed Pearl Harbour and became enemies with the UK, Jocelyn's ship disappeared. As all communication between Britain and Japan was severed, the British War Office was unable to locate such ships, and no word was ever heard again from her wonderful brother, Jocelyn.

Patti with her best friend, Valerie Romaine

As a child, Patti was surrounded by music and developed her love of jazz and performing by listening to the popular sounds of the day, like Duke Ellington, Ella Fitzgerald, Sarah Vaughan, and by watching her mentor Vic Parker, the legendary jazz guitarist from Tiger Bay, who encouraged Patti to sing from an early age.

From the 1960s to the 1980s, Patti honed her craft in the clubs and theatres around the UK and became a seasoned international cabaret artiste. One of the many highlights of Patti's career was appearing as an understudy to the singer, Elaine Delmar, in the hit West End Show, *Bubbling Brown Sugar*.

During the mid-1980s, Patti moved to Spain and became a respected music producer and radio presenter with her shows, *Just for You* and *Costa Nights*. However, Patti never forgot her Tiger Bay roots and returned to Cardiff to perform and create her popular shows, *Jazz Ladies of the Twentieth Century,* and *A Trip Down Memory* Lane, featuring the music of great American composers, and the *Butetown Bay Divas*, with fellow performers, Humie and Jacky Webbe.

For over 60 years, Patti performed jazz to diverse audiences. She worked in different parts of the world, but in recent decades, focused on Cardiff, performing on a voluntary basis to great acclaim in concerts staged in venues ranging from community buildings to the Wales Millennium Centre. She also performed in charity concerts for the local community that were always sold out well in advance.

Patti was a great supporter of the arts and worked tirelessly to ensure that the people behind the music were remembered, recognised and celebrated. One highlight of Patti's career was establishing the popular Butetown Bay Jazz Heritage Festival with her friend and colleague, Humie, which celebrates the musical heritage of Tiger Bay and showcases new up-and-coming musical talent.

In addition to her professional singing career, throughout her life, Patti used her musical talent in the interests of a wide range of good causes. Her music helped bring together people from very different backgrounds and raised awareness of Wales' BME heritage and history. She made a considerable and rich contribution to the work of

Patti and Humie Webbe at the Butetown Bay Jazz Heritage Festival, 2010

Butetown History and Arts Centre over many years, using music and storytelling to work with school groups and providing songwriting workshops for young people, for whom she was a wonderful role model.

As well as performing, Patti loved writing and was passionate about researching Black history and culture. Her book, *Fractured Horizon,* with the photographer, Matthew Manning, and produced in Welsh and English by Butetown History and Arts Centre in 2003, is a look at the memories and changes of Cardiff docklands. Patti also hosted her own radio show on Cardiff Radio, consistently raising broader public awareness of the positive part that the BME community has played in the cultural, economic and social development of Wales.

While in her 70s, Patti received an invitation via the BBC's *Women's Hour* programme to study at the prestigious Ruskin College in Oxford, where she completed two research projects, 'From a Seaside Town to Capital City' about Cardiff, and 'Colouring History', about putting famous women of colour back into history. She was also an advocate and campaigner for Black History to be included on the curriculum, and in 2017, Patti was honoured as one of the founding members of the Black History Month movement in Wales, to which she made regular contributions. In 2019, she was given an EMWWAA Lifetime Achievement Award.

Patti was, above all, a strong woman and mother and faced many challenges throughout her life. In addition to having lost her father and two brothers in the Second World War, she also lost her youngest son, Sean, in a tragic accident. Patti subsequently developed empathy for other families and went on to champion the underdog, and was a dynamic social campaigner. In later years, Patti also worked with members of the community with dementia, raising money for this cause, as well as providing support for sickle-cell disease.

Another of Patti's lifetime causes was to raise awareness of the contributions and sacrifices that ethnic minority members of the Armed Forces and the Merchant Navy made during both world wars. Patti felt people of colour had been forgotten, and she launched a 26-year campaign for a commemorative memorial to recognise the sacrifices of those from minority backgrounds who had fought and died in these wars. Her efforts were finally rewarded in 2019, when a plaque to commemorate the sacrifices of all servicemen and women of colour from Commonwealth countries was unveiled at the Welsh National War Memorial in Cardiff by the Welsh Government and senior officials from the British Armed forces.

Even in her 80s, Patti was still very active in the community, Black history and the arts and remained proud

Patti receiving an EMWWAA Lifetime Achievement Award, 2019

Patti with friend, Humie, on a jazz cruise, c.2003

of her Welsh-Jamaican heritage and her Tiger Bay roots. At the time of her death, she was working on her memoirs, *Born Down My Tiger Bay,* telling the story of the Cardiff docklands and focusing on the lives, sacrifices and determination of the diverse community living there. Patti had recorded the first instalment of an audio CD, and her story will continue through her family and friends, who will contribute their own stories and reflections to complete the book.

Patti sadly lost her short battle with cancer on 10 September 2020, aged 83. She was a beloved mother to Paula and Michael, grandmother to Paul, Ruby, Noah, and great-grandmother to Ezra and Illias. A much loved and respected member of the cultural arts and heritage community, Patti is saluted for her talents as a campaigner, singer, performer, writer, author, promoter, presenter, activist, icon and original Bay diva. Her life is celebrated as an inspirational and dynamic force of energy and someone who will be missed by those who were privileged to know and love her.

# Delivering Justice

## Justna Muhith
**PHARMACOLOGIST AND JUSTICE ADVOCATE**

*I always imagined equality, justice, and inclusion were somebody else's issues to tackle. It's only very late in life that I realised that to make the world a better place, you have to be that difference and to represent.*

I was born in Bangladesh and came to the UK when I was about six months old. My mum was a housewife, and my dad worked in a restaurant and later owned one. I have three brothers and sisters and spent my early years in Splott, Cardiff, being the only ethnic minority family in the area. We were very lucky, as we had great, courageous neighbours who defended us from those who made it their business to hurl abuse and make our lives tough. It was my mum's curries that initially brought the neighbours together, and eventually, we would get invites to join the neighbours' families at Christmas, Easter and other ceremonial events.

As young British citizens growing up, our identities were always in conflict, and we always had an identity crisis. Were we British, Asian, Bangladeshi or Welsh? Homelife was very patriarchal, but the external world was more inclusive and encouraged women to stand up for themselves. It was hard to find a common acceptable etiquette between the different societies.

At primary school, we were the only people of colour, and in Splott, the only family from a Muslim background. When I turned ten, we moved to Roath, a predominately Asian-populated area. It was my parents' search for a more inclusive community where they were better represented and which enabled them to protect their faith that drove their decision to move house.

Moving to Roath was an upheaval, as it changed my whole world and the acceptable social norms. From being able to wear dresses that fell just below the knee with short socks and engaging in Western celebrations, I had to suddenly change my attire to wear trousers under my dress, cover my head, and stay away from too many adult clubbing, partying or pub activities. My social circle was confined to schoolmates during school hours. I wasn't allowed out or encouraged to watch TV or listen to music or speak English at home. From the age of fourteen, I learnt to cook, clean, be obedient, and not question patriarchal domination, adhere to cultural norms and stay away from mainstream media, activities and initiatives. As young adults, you want to engage, explore and be inquisitive, but conflicting societal merits made every day a challenge.

Justna with her parents and brother, Shamim, on a family trip in Bangladesh, shortly before her resolute return to the UK to complete her A levels, 1989

Our parents and grandparents' generations really got stuck in a time lock from the days when they came over to the UK from their homeland. My first visit to Bangladesh as a fourteen-year-old teenager really opened up my eyes. Upon arrival, I was in awe, as the girls there had short hair, attended school wearing skirts and knee socks, and engaged in all the things which were frowned upon for me, even though I was considered to be raised in a progressive Western culture. I felt cheated, while my parents were horrified, as they didn't quite fit in anymore. They soon realised that Bengalis in the UK lead a very confined and isolated life, and they had to re-educate themselves. Growing up, I watched kids fight with their parents because of the societal disparities and change their clothes en route to school and return home in cultural attire. Children were conflicted with themselves and their parents and didn't fit into either society.

At school, I so longed to belong, take part, be understood and be included. At home and at the mosque, we would get scolded for doing things wrong, yet at school, the same behaviours were rewarded. At the mosque, girls went covered up, looked down when spoken to and did not make eye contact, nor challenge authority, but at school, it was all the opposite. Mosque teachings were given respect, honour and privilege, where obedience and female submission was rewarded, but at school, GCSEs, exams and higher education were deemed to be an honour, a privilege and a reward. So my school days were quite lonely, isolating, and I remained quiet, not asking questions so as not to attract attention to myself. It was only at sixth form that a group of us came together from different backgrounds, such as Pakistani, Bengali, Italian, Persian and Chinese, with a few white minority friends joining us too.

Somehow, by the grace of Allah, I managed to get through my GCSEs. I loved art, but as it was deemed a non-rewarding subject, unlike law or medicine, I dropped it after GCSE level. My A levels were primarily scientific subjects, and as I had no place for exam preparations, I had to study behind my grandmother's shadow as she prayed on her mat. No one understood why I wanted to study so badly, but my grandmother gave me some alone time as she prayed. She'd always respected the written text and dedicated years to reading the Quran, so she really tried to relate.

Justna, age 16, with her grandmother, the woman who gave her strength and always believed in her

Attending college was frowned upon, so I stayed at sixth form, and to appease my parents, I had to attend the closest university to home, taking the shortest course available. After qualifying with a BSc pharmacology degree at Cardiff University, I went on to work there at the School of Biosciences as a researcher. The data analysis and writing up of the publications inspired me to seek a Master's.

I applied to Bristol University and was offered a PhD prize studentship. By this point in my life, my dad had started to feel quietly proud that a female in his family had a degree and was dreaming big. At twenty years old, I moved to Bristol. It was very intimidating, and the world was overwhelming and scary, but luckily, I made some lifelong friends along the way. To pay off student debts and to reinforce that I hadn't abandoned my parents, I maintained a weekend job at Woolworths in Cardiff, working from 8am–6pm, while Friday to Sunday nights, I used to help my dad in his restaurant.

In 2002, my father passed away, and our whole world crumbled. My mum drowned in depression, enclosed in a dark room for months, with no idea of how the mortgage or basic bills were going to be paid. The family had no income, so as well as arranging my father's funeral, costs and repatriation to Bangladesh, I suddenly became the head of the family with no time to even grieve myself. I grew up fast literally overnight, and I'd only lost my grandmother a few months before that.

Tutoring served as my therapy to help overcome depression. I gave back to others the joy of education and the value of independence that I was not privy to. I took on an additional job tutoring children of low-income households, as well as women from communities around Bristol that ordinarily didn't like to engage. I tutored in science subjects and coached students with their university applications. I counselled and convinced parents that education for a female gives independence and honour and enables a future for the child and their whole family.

I have a very proud and vivid memory of a Somalian family whose mother was so honoured that a Black–Asian girl studying for her PhD could be a role model for her kids. Today, this family has a member who's gone on to study international law, obtaining a first-class degree. Another sister and her brother have completed a Bachelor's in biomedical sciences, going on to graduate with a Master's. My other students went on to do subjects such as veterinary sciences, medicine, pharmacy, marine biology, nursing, teaching and many more subjects. I never consciously ever set out to make such a difference to people's lives and society, but I am very pleased that I did.

My main career has been in pharmaceuticals, which I embarked on after leaving Bristol, moving to London. A few years later, identity conflict, societal pressures and self-loathing of guilt for being selfish and wanting an education and independence over my parents' wish for me to get married to a man of their choice finally caught up with me. I succumbed to marrying a man with no visa or degree and with no dignity or respect for a woman with a voice. Over the next few years, I became a fraction of my former self.

Justna working as a medical advisor in the pharmaceutical industry from her home office, 1999

In the interim, between writing up my PhD and joining the pharmaceutical industry, I worked as a personal development coach, helping women who had entered the UK as spouses of men who treated them inappropriately and prevented them from learning the language and integrating into society. I became their voice, eyes and ears, and in that role, I helped many vulnerable women to escape from domestic violence. Little did I know, years later, I would fall foul of the same.

I was torn between a society that forbade divorce and a society that condemns domestic abuse. Divorce was torturous, like living every moment of the marriage all over again. But Allah truly works in mysterious ways. Three weeks after I filed for divorce, I got offered a job in Germany.

In Germany, I lived on the waterfront region of Hafeninsel, and my two girls went to an international school. My independence meant that I could afford a good life and standard of living for my kids, even in a foreign country. But I spent months being very depressed, crying

Justna with daughters, Eliza, 3 and Enysha, 18 months

and staring into the midnight sky, watching the water roll on by, and people enjoying music from my balcony window after I'd put the kids to sleep. The irony is that my PhD was about studying models of anxiety, fear and depression. One night, while watching the glistening stars, I realised that I could not afford to lose myself now. My kids would have no one, and their lives would regress into the society I tried to pull myself out of, so I had to be strong and pick myself up.

Going through court, I uncovered so many gaps in my basic knowledge of UK law and began to learn about matrimonial law on the internet. One night, I came across a law conversion course. It appealed to me because I could acquire knowledge on different legislations impacting family life and the division of assets. After finishing the first year of law and finalising my divorce, I decided I had something to offer the judiciary by way of a different societal perspective, and so in 2019, I got sworn in as a magistrate.

Most of my personal time is now dedicated to voluntary work. I sit as a board member on Women's Connect First in Cardiff, help raise awareness of ethnic inequity as a Healthcare Businesswomen's Association Ethnicity Affinity Group director, and am part of the Women in STEM education subcommittee.

My life's education gave me the freedom to be 'me' and to be self-sufficient. My dad's favourite saying that, 'It's

Justna with daughter Enysha, receiving an EMWWAA award for contributions to science, technology and healthcare, 2019

never too late to self-educate, and no one can take those accomplishments from you', influenced my life-long learning. My life certainly took a U-turn from being a shy, coy, reserved, quiet young girl who was humiliated in class and told 'you will be a failure in life' by her sociology teacher, a subject in which I later excelled, to today being a voice, mentor and role model for many.

A true leader's impact cannot be counted, and their influence cannot be measured. It's like a stone thrown into a pond—the ripple is you, whose impact cannot be seen, but it can surely be felt by those whom you've touched. We shouldn't always expect to always fit in, but we should aim to create our own space, break boundaries, lead with empathy, bring people together, and actively 'be that change'. Imparting our knowledge may create the greatest legacy we leave behind, but no one will ever know unless we take part.

# Enacting Positive Change

## Rocio Cifuentes
**CEO OF ETHNIC MINORITIES AND YOUTH SUPPORT TEAM, WALES**

*Change doesn't happen unless you change things.*
*You have to be that change and ask questions and be willing to take a risk and try something new.*

I was born in Santiago, in Chile, in the middle of Pinochet's dictatorship. My parents were students, but they were quite active politically in opposing the dictatorship. After I was born, things became harder for them, and they didn't want to put my life at risk by staying in Chile, so they decided to leave.

There was a charity called the World University Service, which supports students who are unable to continue their studies in their home countries for political reasons. Together with the United Nations High Commission for Refugees, they organised places in various universities around the world where exiled students from Chile could continue their studies. My parents had a choice between going to Sweden or Swansea and, as they didn't speak any Swedish, they chose Swansea. I was a baby when we came to Wales, and my brother was born there when I was three.

I grew up in quite a nice part of Swansea. My parents finished their studies, and soon after they graduated, they managed to get good jobs, so my life was quite nice. We

Rocio with her parents, age 2

weren't well off, but we never lacked for anything. I enjoyed school and was quite academic. I was just a regular Welsh girl and had lots of friends, both Welsh and Chilean.

At that time in Swansea, there was a small community of Chilean people, around thirty or forty families who were like my extended family of aunties, uncles and cousins. I kept hearing my parents talk about what had happened and that they were political refugees from Chile. I don't remember feeling any stigma or embarrassment. I think the word refugee didn't carry the same negative connotations that it has today. Fortunately for me, I just thought it was a way of explaining who I was and why I was in Wales.

Although I had a regular upbringing, I guess I always understood that an injustice had been done to my parents and to other Chilean people, and that they were still fighting and struggling to put that situation right. There was a large movement of Chileans who were exiled and challenging the dictatorship, and there was quite a big, ongoing activist movement throughout my childhood.

Because I spoke Spanish and I'd started to learn French in school and enjoyed languages, there were teachers who said I should work somewhere like the UN. So I considered it, or some kind of context where I would use my languages, but for a social purpose. Before I went to university, I had a gap year and went to Chile for a year. I really got to know where my parents came from, and for the first time, I understood why they ate certain things and why they talked a certain way. Everything about the way they were finally made sense.

I went to university in Cambridge and studied political science. It was a great experience, and it really opened my eyes to the extent of inequality and extremes of wealth and poverty that exist in the UK. After I graduated, I lived in London for a short time, but I didn't really enjoy it, as it was just too big, impersonal and exhausting on a practical level. It wasn't the way I was used to living in Cambridge or Swansea, and it was too disconnected. You could go for days without seeing any friends.

I didn't really plan to come back to Swansea, but I did. Swansea is a very small, close-knit community, and you knew everybody. I had friends from growing up who were still in Swansea, and it was a life I was quite familiar with. I worked briefly at Swansea University in the Public Policy Research Department, and race and ethnicity were some of the topics that I worked on there.

But I also didn't really like being too academic and too detached from reality, so I left the university, and for a few years, went to work in a charity that supports young people at risk of homelessness. I wanted to do something more hands-on and more real, so other than a few years teaching and a few years doing research at university, I've always consistently worked in the charity sector. I guess I just want to help and do good, and I couldn't ever see myself working for any other purpose.

I was always interested in ethnicity, and in university, I did various modules on race and ethnicity. Racism was something that I'd always associated with the UK or the West, of white people being racist against Black or brown people. One of the things that shocked me when I went to Chile was that Chilean people were actually extremely racist to the indigenous people, and it really surprised me that a people could be racist against themselves.

So ethnicity was something that I started to question as being quite subjective and which changed, depending on the situation. For example, when I went to Chile, people didn't think I was Chilean—they saw me as British. So I started to really think about identity, and I carried that through when I came back to Wales, thinking about the concept of Welshness. My Master's research topic was about how young people defined Welshness and how ethnicity came into play. My hypothesis was that Welsh identity is more ethnically fluid than English or British and potentially more inclusive.

When I was in my late 20s, I was contacted by an old school friend to apply for a job at a charity called the Council of Ethnic Minority Voluntary Organisations, which was a UK-wide operation looking to set up in Wales, and they wanted someone to help them. So I applied, not really thinking I would get it because I didn't really have experience specifically in the third sector. But they hired me, and in that role, I came across a struggling youth group, which was the pilot project of what became Ethnic

EYST full team

Minorities and Youth Support Team Wales (EYST). I helped them constitute it and have just learnt as I've gone along.

Now, as the CEO, I oversee the whole organisation and develop partnerships with stakeholders, Welsh and local government, and public bodies. I also manage a team consisting of 60 people who work in various offices across Wales—in Wrexham, Newport, Cardiff and in the EYST-owned premises in Swansea that include offices, a youth and community centre and a new bespoke advice hub for those seeking sanctuary.

I also devise projects, seek funding for them and oversee their delivery while making sure the organisation runs legally, safely and in line with our charitable objectives. We operate a multilingual helpline, provide support for resettled refugees, and have a project across Wales to help Black and minority ethnic children and young people.

We're trying to make a difference to people's lives, and that can be in a very practical way. For example, if we have a job, we do our best to give it to someone with all the skills and expertise needed, but also with lived experience of the issue needing to be addressed. We also try and create projects that respond to the need people have for education, jobs or skills, so we have a lot of volunteering programmes.

It's been really enjoyable working at EYST, as it's been driven from the heart, and I've been lucky to have worked from the very beginning with a group of people who are also driven by the same values, vision and passion. We're like a family, and I've realised that it's the people that you have in a team that actually make you successful. Some of the more recent challenges have been due to the organisation having grown quite significantly in the past few years, so when you're so big and not seeing people every day, maintaining that family feel can be a challenge.

There have also been some practical challenges on certain occasions, and the politics of the sector has also not been particularly pleasant to deal with. But in the end, I've just learned to really trust my instincts and remain true to myself, and stick with my values and what I believe. We're trying to make a difference on the ground, so rather than giving too much time and energy to petty politics that happen, competing for funding, status, and power, putting our values first is what we try and do.

The way I get inspired to carry on working— because it is hard work and the pay's not fantastic in the charity sector—is that I really enjoy listening to people directly.

Rocio as Chair of the Welsh Refugee Coalition at the Sanctuary at the Senedd event, 2018

128 SEVENTY YEARS OF STRUGGLE AND ACHIEVEMENT

When you meet with a Welsh Government minister, it's obvious what's missing is an actual service or mechanism to connect with the people, so I try and create projects that bridge the massive gap.

It's something that I'm really driven by, to the extent that my partner thinks that I never stop working, because I'm constantly reading about ethnicity, race or poverty at the weekends. But I guess it's just my life and it's what I'm interested in. I would love to continue to lead EYST and see it continue to grow and help people and make a difference, but I would also like to explore the potential of doing something slightly different, but I really don't know.

Receiving the EMWWAA Social and Humanitarian Achievement award in 2019 was a huge honour, and it was really touching to be recognised in the humanitarian category because, above everything else, what I feel that I am is a humanitarian. So, I don't just try and advocate for ethnic minority rights or women's rights or refugees; as to me, it's about everybody. The experience was humbling, and I dedicated the award to my parents in my acceptance speech because of their struggles and what they went through, and because their hardships have translated into my success, and I wouldn't be here without them.

I suppose anything is possible. But I think what I've learnt is that most people don't know very much more than you

Rocio with husband, John and children, Mia and Zefi

or me. You assume that there are experts and people who are very knowledgeable about the world, politics, and systems, but it really isn't the case. People are quite clueless and just trying to get by day to day. So, I think people should be more confident to voice their concerns or to ask questions if something doesn't make sense because the likelihood is that if it doesn't make sense to one person, it probably doesn't make sense to lots of people. So don't be afraid to ask questions and challenge things because change doesn't happen unless you change things. You have to be that change and ask those questions and be willing to take a risk and try something new. Otherwise, we're just going to be the same forever.

# Life Flow

## Madhvi Dalal
**FOUNDER, PADMAD**

*Perhaps I am like water. The secrets of the ocean were always in the drop of water. I just needed to flow through an unknown path.*

I was born and brought up in Eldoret, in a wonderful corner of Kenya. I went to a British school and grew up as a quiet, dutiful Indian girl. Within the confusion of these different cultures, I was constantly trying to understand all the subtle things Mother Nature had to offer: Does the caterpillar feel something deep inside which tells her she will be a butterfly? Does the ice from the mountains know that nothing, yet everything will change through its journey?

As I grew slightly older, I left home to study in the more modern and fast-growing city of Nairobi. Living without my parents from the age of twelve, life was dynamic, and things around me were changing all the time. As I waded through adolescence, I tried to achieve as much as I could. I also immersed myself in Bharatanatyam, a traditional form of dance. Dance scaffolded me through my growth and required courage, hard work, stamina and above all, discipline. I learned how to learn. Until then, it felt as though I was covered in a protective, shiny, slimy covering, hanging and looking at life upside down. Dance transformed me, and perhaps it was my time to emerge as a butterfly.

My sister had gone to Cardiff to study optometry at the university, so I also went to Cardiff University to study pharmacy. The course was the exact opposite of what I was craving, as it was dull, but safe. However, the city was exciting and vibrant. I made friends, who were my rocks, and I got used to living in Wales, even climbing mountains capped with snow. During my days in university, I really felt like I had colourful wings and had found freedom. I was also finding my way in little and large achievements. I performed Bharatanatyam dance at student cultural events, including at Bath and Bristol universities, as well as at City Hall, and was interviewed by the BBC for my contributions to dance in Wales.

Madhvi performing a solo dance show at the Kala Academy in Goa, India, 1997

After qualifying as a pharmacist, I eventually moved to Kent, where I worked at Boots. I found my journey to independence very fulfilling. I liked my job, my home and my little car. I also matured and found my voice, developing an armour. I gravitated towards women's rights and started becoming a voice for them, which I expressed through dance, performing in prestigious places in India, Australia and Europe.

By this time, I had met Chirav, who was also a pharmacist. He was expressive, vibrant and full of words – the opposite of me. Nevertheless, after a few adventures together, we got together and married in my home town, Eldoret, in 2002.

Life became hectic, though we felt at home in Wales. We bought a pharmacy in Pontnewynydd and started working harder than ever before. Just as we bought it, the government closed the GP surgery directly connected with it. We couldn't pull out and had to face the consequences of the business taking a nosedive before we had even started. Thankfully, with Chirav's gift of the gab and my organisational skills, we managed to trudge through. As our business grew, we bought a post office across the road. Just as we were finding our way, the government decided to close the post office. Once again, our business began to nose dive, though we once more put in a 200 per cent effort.

Madhvi and colleagues, having won the Pharmacy Practice of the Year award at the National Pharmacy Awards, 2011

In the meantime, Chirav had developed rheumatoid arthritis, which was a big blow, and quickly left him very debilitated. The mental and emotional trauma seemed much more overwhelming than the physical symptoms, and it was very tough to watch. Chirav opted to go down the path of Ayurvedic treatment and left for India, where he stayed for three years. I faced a terrifying, uncertain future, but I carried on working hard and made it through with the help of our committed staff. In seven years, we won six awards, our biggest accolade being the Pharmacy Practice of the Year award in 2011, a real endorsement of our achievements against the odds.

Through this period, my dance career flourished too. I secured grants from the Arts Council of Wales and performed at the opening of the glossy Newport Arts Centre, the Chapter Arts Centre in Cardiff, and many other places. I collaborated, created, performed, choreographed and taught. All of this earned me two Welsh Asian Woman Achievement Awards, one in Arts in 2011 and one in Business in 2013.

In 2010, we had our first daughter. We named her Neeyati, which means 'destiny'. Learning how to look after a baby was challenging, as apparently, babies don't come with manuals. But between Google and our amazing nanny and family, we made it through the seasons, and Neeyati grew up with a warm, Welsh accent.

As soon as I saw a small gap between work, the baby and chores, I decided to get trained as a yoga instructor. My course was over several months and in London, but the yoga teacher was inspirational, and I loved what I was learning. I qualified with a diploma, and when I was pregnant with our second baby, I specialised in prenatal yoga and did a qualification based in Cambridge.

Through this period, we decided to uproot and move to Kenya, which was a tough and emotional decision. Wales was home for us and a place where we felt secure, and where we had seemingly achieved a lot. However, Chirav's health condition had worsened in the damp climate. We were also getting disillusioned with the excesses of the First World and felt we should move to the Third World to see where we could help. So, we decided to sell up and move to Nairobi.

Madhvi practicing yoga at Hob House, Nairobi, 2021

In the meantime, things were busy, and I'd been overworking too much. While pregnant with our daughter, Aaditi, I developed HELLP, a life-threatening type of pre-eclampsia, and I nearly died and almost lost Aaditi too. Thanks to the staff at Royal Gwent Hospital, we survived and were ready to face the world.

We arrived in Nairobi for our new lives when Aadi was only six weeks old. She was a different child than Neeyati, so motherhood again came with its challenges. Fortunately, with the help of family, friends and the sunshine, we managed to find our footing. Chirav and I sat the incredibly difficult pharmacy exams so we would have a safety net. I started teaching yoga for kids in schools and found myself on the International Yoga Day committee and as an instructor at the world-famous Lamu Yoga Festivals.

I also joined my former teacher's dance class, which was held every Saturday and Sunday afternoons for three hours. The commitment to the class and preparing for performances was immense, and the guilt of leaving the kids for hours every weekend was even worse. Chirav had started a business in Eldoret, which was 400 km from where we lived, and I was a single parent with the girls for nearly three years.

During this time, I began teaching dance in the slums as a volunteer for Moving Cultures, a community-based cultural activism movement focused on utilising the power of the arts to make a positive change around the world. During one of my trips, I remember expressing my feeling of disconnect to the founder, as I was finding difficulty with things like financial and gender inequality, racial exclusion, corruption and inconsistencies in education. I was told not to moan about it but to do something instead, which is what I chose to do.

One of the things I came face to face with in the slums was period poverty, so I decided to travel around Kenya to understand the problem in more depth and to document my findings. I remember a real turning point when we were filming in a slum in Nairobi, and I asked one of the residents of the orphanage where she got her sanitary wear from and discovered that she used to give regular sexual favours to a teacher who would pay her with packs of sanitary

Madhvi conducting a workshop for kids in Kakamega. The partnership will help more than 4,000 girls in the area

pads. However, she didn't want to be rescued by child protection services because she said she was okay since she had food, water and shelter. I also discovered that 65% of women and girls in Kenya cannot afford pads and miss several school days each month as a result, and also that many girls go into transactional sex in exchange for pads.

From then, I began to work very hard on developing a product that was comfortable and functional, as well as being economical, durable, healthy and environmentally friendly. I started educating boys and girls in schools on

Madhvi with daughters, Aaditi and Neeyati; husband, Chirav and her parents at a family wedding, 2021

Madhvi with PadMad advocate, Eliud Kipchoge, a record-breaking marathon runner and athletics legend, who leads by his motto: 'No human is limited', Eldoret, 2020

menstrual health management and sexual and reproductive health rights. I listened to many stories, each more heart-wrenching than the last.

As I collated feedback from pilot schemes, I managed to brand PadMad, a reusable sanitary pad, as a social enterprise. PadMad began to get much traction very quickly as the press started featuring me and my work, thus further spreading the awareness. Within two years, I won a few awards, one of them being a Power Woman of the Year award. I also began attracting celebrities to act as ambassadors for the initiative and started working closely with the government of Kenya to standardise reusable sanitary products.

My enthusiasm, courage and focus got stronger, and I

found myself working on the ground almost every day. My voice became louder as I heard more and more distressing stories from girls and women. I advocate strongly and sometimes fight for gender equality, positive environmental impact, health awareness, as well as education and basic human rights. I am often called a feminist, but I prefer to be known as an equalist instead.

Currently, PadMad is a leading brand in combatting period poverty in Kenya, as well as parts of Africa and Asia. Life has a whole new meaning for me now, as there is an intense satisfaction in what I do. Many say that I do good for others, but I feel the others are doing good for me at a much more spiritual level.

I am now settled in Nairobi with Chirav and our two young girls, who are already developing their own tools to help the world through mindfulness and awareness of period poverty. The sun shines every day, and the grass gets greener.

Perhaps I am like water. The secrets of the ocean were always in the drop of water. I just needed to flow through an unknown path.

# Positive Educational Exchange

## Christina Roy
**FAMILY LEARNING COORDINATOR, PARENT LEARNING GROUP, CATHAYS HIGH SCHOOL, CARDIFF COUNCIL**

*I feel I belong to both Western and Eastern cultures, and I think I fit in well, wherever I am. If you're a positive person, when you are with other people, you spread your positivity.*

I was born in London on Christmas Day, 1976, to an Indian family. We went back to India when I was three, as my parents decided we needed to learn about our traditions, culture and language. Settling in India wasn't too bad for me because I joined the school and just went with the flow. We were in India for 21 years with my working parents and my elder brother. Both my parents were my role models and have passed on many skills to my brother and me, of which we are proud. Another role model in my life was my tutor, who was also a friend and like an elder sister to me.

When we came back to the UK in 2002, I had already graduated with an Honours degree in geography from a college in Calcutta, and had a diploma in travel and tourism management. I decided to shift to a new career in education, as I felt it would be more suitable for family life. I was offered a teaching assistant job straight away, which opened up new ways of learning for me, which were very different from the Indian style of teaching and education. I worked with primary schools in London with learners of English as an Additional Language (EAL). This made me realise that I could use my language skills to build up my career, so I started teaching Bengali as a community language.

Even though my parents were Indian nationals, they originated from Bangladesh, and my family arranged my marriage with a qualified doctor from Bangladesh who had settled in the UK. We started our lives together in December 2003, like any other struggling young couple in a foreign country. Fortunately, we were both hard-working, compatible and had positive natures. Through my husband's work as a doctor, we moved from London in 2007 and settled down in Wales, in Haverfordwest, Brecon, and finally Cardiff three years later.

I then started a teaching assistant job in Cathays High

School, which was a change from teaching in a primary school. I specialised in working with students with autism and special learning needs, and I enjoyed working for many years in that position. I also taught Bengali as a modern foreign language at a GCSE-level club.

I'd always had an inner desire to do a post-graduate degree in teaching and was lucky enough that, while working at the school, they allowed me to study part-time at Cardiff Metropolitan University. I was so fortunate to have had their support and encouragement, as well as from my husband, family and friends. Otherwise, I would not have been able to do it. I completed my PGCE in 2017, and soon after, was offered a promotion as a family learning coordinator in a teaching role in Cathays High School. I also work as a senior examiner for an exam board for GCSE and A level Bengali as a community language, which helps keep me connected to my roots.

Christina (*second from the left*) with the Parent Learning Group, receiving an Inspire Closing the Gap Community Award, 2018

I always felt that I needed to pass on the knowledge and skills that I had learnt. In 2014, I created a parent learning group within Cathays High School. I think we were the first in Cardiff to create such a group. Even though the group started small, there are now around 50 learners each term, mostly women, and from all over the world, like Bangladesh, India, Spain, Japan and Italy. In 2018, we took part in a reading challenge in collaboration with the Cardiff libraries, which showed that as the parents' reading improved, so did their children's, so it's definitely having an impact. Recently, both the deputy minister and the education minister visited our parent learning group virtually and praised our work highly. The importance of family learning for children has proven itself well, so hopefully, in the near future, a framework will be created to spread it out to all schools in Wales.

As the family learning group grew, I realised that I wanted to build the confidence of these ladies to be a positive role model for their children and to positively impact their children's education. So on top of running a reading group, we moved on to basic literacy skills and, then, worked in partnership with Adult Learning Cardiff and Cardiff Metropolitan University to introduce accredited courses alongside English language (ESOL) qualifications.

My next project was getting these women into employment, so we collaborated and partnered with other organisations, like Dewis CIL and Cardiff Council, and started getting people extra qualifications in things like food hygiene and first aid, which led to getting them enrolled into agencies. We have about ten women who

Christina receiving an EMWWAA certificate from Welsh First Minister Mark Drakeford as a finalist in the Self-Development category

Christina celebrating New Year's Eve with her family: Dr Anjan Roy, daughter, Orchita and son, Onkon, 2019

have now gone back to work as carers, kitchen assistants or in other services. I feel quite pleased that I have been an inspiration to other women in helping them to become educated, more confident and empowered and to get a new lease in life.

That was a brilliant start for my career, and then on top of that, we won an Inspire Award in 2018, which was our first national recognition. I feel I have achieved more than I wanted because I never thought of getting an award, but it happened, especially because of the people who supported me. I was then nominated for an Inspire Tutor Award and also nominated in 2018 for the EMWWAA Award for Self-Development.

I am still doing things for my learners wherever possible. If I see anyone who is willing and motivated to get into work, I will guide them. If I can't do something, I will signpost them to other people, but I will make sure that they reach their destination. So that gives me inner happiness because when I see other people achieving, it makes me feel that I have done something for someone.

In 2020, through a British Council Connecting Classroom project, I had also been able to virtually visit places like a girls' college in Bangladesh, and to discuss global issues like water resources. So I've been able to connect and empower women from around the world, which has been a completely different experience for me.

Education and skills can't be taken away from anyone, and it's something that if I pass on to someone, then they can pass it on to more people, and that way, it will expand. If someone new comes to Cardiff, I would suggest that they try and enrich themselves and that there are a lot of free courses to make use of. They also need the self-confidence to believe in themselves and build on their skills, step by step, to reach their goals and dreams, which are then achievable.

Another dream of mine was to have my own family. My husband is my best companion and understands and supports me in my life. He himself is a successful psychiatrist and a self-made man. We also live with my elderly in-laws, which gives me an opportunity to take care of them. I have a handsome thirteen-year-old son and a beautiful eight-year-old daughter, and they are both doing well as young achievers in life. My son is a chorister with Llandaff Cathedral and loves his musical training. As my children were both born in Wales, they have adapted more of the Welsh culture alongside the traditions and values of our own culture.

I am very proud of my family but also the community that I belong to and the work I do for them. I contribute wherever I can and cannot say no to people. I am part of the Wales Puja Committee, where I work as a voluntary catering officer, organising all the meals for the Puja ritual days and feeding up to 300 to 400 people on an annual basis. Within that organisation, I've also had many opportunities to run educational projects with children.

Christina and her husband celebrating Durga Puja, an annual Bengali Hindu festival, 2019

I have never faced racism for being an Asian woman. I think that the community out here has been supportive of my being an ethnic minority. I feel that I belong to both cultures of West and East, and my aim is to sustain both cultures. I speak Bengali at home and follow all traditions and customs from my Hindu background.

One of my recent projects was very interesting, run in conjunction with Cathays Heritage Library. Parents shared stories of

Christina demonstrating her passion for cooking and serving the community

their cultures, festivals and traditions, and how they moved from their own countries and sustained these practices while also adapting Welsh culture, amalgamating both. We also ran a creative session with women from around the world, embroidering different cushion covers. All those cushions and stories were displayed in the Story Museum of Cardiff. Our most recent activity was involving some parent volunteers with the Food4All project, collecting unwanted food from supermarkets and donating it to families in need. The project is aimed at making Wales more sustainable.

I am a diabetic champion with Diabetes UK and a dementia champion with the Alzheimer's Society, and I spread awareness through various workshops. I also run cookery lessons, which sometimes involve Welsh cooking. I have been involved with many projects with a variety of communities in Cardiff to spread positivity. I'm a very positive person, and wherever I go, I think I spread my positivity.

Every woman is born with some qualities, and through the years, they develop many skills. To get into work, they need to use their skills and sometimes reskill themselves, depending on the needs of the community. But once a woman starts valuing herself, then she can achieve many things. Every woman can be a homemaker, but they should all showcase their own skills in order to make their mark in the world.

# Shining a Light on Culture

## Wai Fong Lee
**FOUNDER AND CHAIR OF THE CHINESE COMMUNITY CO-OP CENTRE**

*From the darkness, you bring people back to see the light. The sunshine is always there, but you can't always see it. When you look at life positively, every day the sun is shining.*

I was born in Hong Kong and lived in a village with my grandmother and two younger brothers. Life was not easy. I had to go to school in the morning and in the afternoon I had to work in a factory to make some money. I also had to do housework and look after my grandmother and brothers, which was not much fun—all work and looking after the family.

I came to the UK in 1975, only thirteen years of age. It wasn't a very nice experience because, at that time, my parents were already in the UK, and I had to travel alone from Hong Kong. My father was working in London and my mother in Cardiff. I had to stay with a relative for six months until we set up a takeaway business in Swansea and the family could reunite there.

It was hard for me and very scary going to school every day, as I couldn't speak any English and couldn't understand what people were saying, and I didn't know anything about the culture. So, every day, I just sat in the corner of the classroom feeling very lonely. Some people discriminated against me, and one day someone smacked me in the face. My father told me just to accept it, as we were living in other people's country with their rules. I felt it was so unfair. We're all human beings, and we're all the same. Why did I have to suffer like this?

This was 1976, and I learned that people from other countries were not respected. They thought we were just coming here to make money, but we work hard and contribute and never claim benefits. But I just had to accept it because even in my own country, maybe I wouldn't have been happy every day either. After I learned a bit of English, I could start to communicate with others and then people were nice to me. I just had to accept the situation, and to try and enjoy it.

I worked in our family's small takeaway business every

day after school, since we were open from 5pm till midnight, seven days a week. I finished my fifth form and wanted to carry on to college. Unfortunately, my father didn't want me to go to college because they couldn't cope without me at work. So, I had to stay in the shop and work for my dad every day, so I had no chance to go to college or university. That was my life until I met my husband. We started our own business, and then I only had to work six days a week and got a day off. Before we had children, we would spend our day off shopping, and afterwards, we would spend the day with the kids.

Wai Fong presenting a cheque of funds raised for the Lord Mayor's Charity by the Swansea Chinese community during their Chinese New Year celebrations, 2006

I think it's important to tell children that not everything is negative and there are positives. We taught our children not to get angry at some people who are just naïve, so they shouldn't take any notice, or it would make things worse. I think, because we couldn't communicate we lost confidence and dignity, and we hid ourselves and didn't talk to other people. But the children have been brought up here, so they could speak the language and communicate with other people, so they didn't face much discrimination. Communication is so important. If you communicate with other people, they treat you as the same kind of human being.

Wai Fong with daughter, Teresa, age 1

In 1997, I founded the Chinese Community Co-op Centre, and I was the chair there until a few years ago. When I first started, I had a lot of criticism from men in the Chinese community about women stepping into the front line instead of being housewives and looking after children. I was upset by the criticism, and my husband was too, but I didn't want to give up because I just wanted to help people who were suffering or in need, so I didn't care what anybody said. I even offered to swap places with some of those who criticised me, but nobody wanted the role, so I stayed there for over 20 years. It's hard work because you've got to have your phone on 24 hours a day because you expect people will call you for help.

I would often take elderly people out on day trips, which they loved. Some of them didn't get on so well with the younger generation, who were born in this country and don't speak our languages or know much about the culture. So, the older generation felt isolated because a lot of them couldn't speak good English because they'd had no chance to learn. Many wanted to talk to a group of people who spoke the same languages.

So, I started planning a project to build a new home for the elderly. I worked with the Family Housing Association, the local government, and also got support from the Welsh Assembly. It took me about four years to plan everything and to build the home called Swan Gardens. It was worth it because we've got 23 flats for elderly people and my parents are living there too. It's right in the centre, not far from the market, and the residents can go shopping. They're living with their own people, who speak their languages, and there are also three Chinese people working there who can help them sort out their problems. It's not easy for them to change their lifestyle when they get to be 60. They just want a quiet life, watching

Wai Fong with Swansea's Lord Mayor cutting the ribbon at the grand opening of Swan Gardens, 2005

Swansea Chinese School Christmas celebration, 1996

television, and we managed to get a Chinese channel for them. So, they've got a very nice life, and I feel grateful to see how the people living there are so happy.

I also formed a Chinese school in Swansea, as I feel it's important for children not to forget their own languages and culture. I've worked regularly with the Confucius Institute Chinese School, and they've now got about 160 children. So, I really feel that's something that is so important for our Chinese people.

I was working so much for the community, I didn't use to have time for religion, but when I retired, I became a Buddhist, and now I enjoy reading Sutras and helping people in a different way. It's like I ended a chapter a few years ago and started a new chapter in my life, which is exciting because I found lots of new things I'd never noticed before, and I've met so many nice people.

Every year I go to Taiwan for a month to do voluntary work at a Buddhist museum. A lot of people come from

A trip organised by the Swansea Co-op Centre for members of the Chinese community, 2016

Wai Fong celebrating Chinese New Year as a volunteer at the Buddha Museum in Taiwan, 2020

different countries and, as not many people who work there can speak English, I help with the tourists. I spend time with them and tell them about the history of the museum and the Buddha. It's nice to feel useful, and I find it very exciting to share everything that I've learned. I think I will treasure every moment of every day of my life.

For many years before I became a Buddhist, I was already connected with the Buddhist way because the Buddha always shows so much compassion, helping others, without asking for anything in return. I believe because I had an unhappy experience and suffered without any help, I don't want to see people suffering. I want to help people and take the pain away from them and to support them, which is what the Buddha says. If people are lost, they have no direction. From the darkness, you bring people back to see the light.

I think as long as you are nice and enjoy your life, there are always nice people around to help you too. It only matters how you see and create your life, so you've got to be strong to face problems and carry on and not give up. The sunshine is always there, but you can't always see it. When you look at life positively, every day the sun is shining.

# Supportive Strength

## Wanjiku Ngotho-Mbugua
**REGIONAL DIRECTOR, BAWSO**

*I make a point of introducing myself to every BME person that I meet and invite them to my offices for a cup of tea. The people I'm supporting are very isolated, and I feel privileged and blessed to be able to help others in this way.*

I was born in a small village in Kenya called Kiambururu, about 30 miles from Nairobi. I was the seventh of nine children, four boys and five girls. My father was a city planner for the city council in Nairobi. He commuted from the village and, as he was one of the few people in the village who had a car, he was regarded as a rich man. My mother was a housewife and took care of us, but she was also very enterprising and did all different kinds of farming. She grew coffee, maize and potatoes and sold them to the markets and coffee factories.

My parents were very religious. They were both Catholics, which was very unusual in my village, where most people were Presbyterians, and there were no Catholic churches in my village. Mass was said in our sitting room with a priest every day, and on days like Good Friday and Easter Sunday, we would walk long distances to the parish church just so that we could join the other parishioners.

When I was growing up, my father made me feel I was very special and told me I was an intelligent person and would go to university and make a good career for myself. So I grew up very confident that I was going to make something of my life because he put so much hope and confidence in me.

I loved reading, and if my sisters couldn't find me, I'd usually be on the side of the road reading a torn-up piece of newspaper. In the village, there wasn't much to do. We had a big field where we played different games with our mates—hide and seek, jump rope, and we went to the river looking for eels. But we didn't have much time to play, as we worked a lot. We were expected to plant and help with the harvesting of coffee and taking it to the factory, about two or three miles away, carrying it on our back. Today, in this country, this would be looked at as child labour, but it wasn't, and it gave us purpose and discipline.

I went to a very good girls' high school run by strict German Catholic Precious Blood sisters, and then went to Nairobi University and studied for a BA in linguistics and literature. I was quite young when I finished university—about nineteen or twenty. I'd also had a baby at university, so afterwards, I went back home with my daughter. I had to get a job quickly to support us, so I started teaching in a high school in a nearby town and stayed for about six years.

Wanjiku, (*second from the left*) with her daughter, Ivy (*in front*), friends and parents (*on either end*), departing on her first trip from Kenya to visit her sister in Ireland, 2000

In the year 2000, I made my first trip to Europe to visit my older sister in Ireland. I liked it so much there, I kept thinking, what can be better than living here? I thought I'd have better opportunities in Europe, so I returned to Ireland at the end of the year with my daughter. The following year, I met my future husband in Ireland, and we travelled and lived in various places like Malaysia, Bangladesh, Dubai and Botswana.

From Botswana, we decided to come to Wales at my husband's request. I'd heard of Wales but had no idea where it was. We found a place in Maesteg and arrived in 2001. I was pregnant with my second daughter at that point. My first daughter, who was six, went to the local school, where she went through really bad racism. We spoke to the teachers about this, and they said there was nothing they could do. We decided to move to Pencoed, and I got a job in a Sony TV factory. I had to leave for work at 6am, but I became friends with some mothers who helped me to take my daughter to school in the morning. My husband eventually left us and returned to Ireland, and my girls and I lived in Pencoed for three or four years, and I got a job with Legal and General in Cardiff.

Wanjiku with husband, Ian and daughters, Sienna, Ivy and Kylie, Christmas Day, 2020

While I was in Cardiff, a friend who had volunteered with Bawso (Black Association of Women Step Out) told me they were recruiting. So I went into work for Bawso in 2005 as a floating support worker, helping a lot of asylum seekers and refugees settled in the Cardiff Bay area with housing and tenancy issues.

In 2006, a job opportunity arose for Bawso in Wrexham. I didn't even know where Wrexham was, but I got the job and ended up moving to Wrexham. I worked so hard and was alone, though I got a few volunteers in the community. And I was able to evidence our work, such that the following year, the Welsh Government funded our work for the first time in Wrexham. We then recruited three support workers and had many volunteers. In 2009, we got funding from the Welsh Government and were able to purchase a building.

The project is working really well. We now have about twelve full-time workers in the project, covering the whole of the six counties of north Wales. The work I do on a daily basis is fighting an ongoing battle for people who've been discriminated against or denied certain rights because of their ethnicity or race. I'm a voice for BME people in north Wales and bringing their issues to policymakers so they can include them.

Wanjiku (*in orange jacket*) pictured with colleagues at Bawso

I've also supported girls that have come from abroad and got married to local men in north Wales, and the marriage has broken down because of domestic abuse or worse, where they've been brought here as sex slaves, or so that the girls can work for the men's businesses and clean for their relatives. Many of these girls are running away from Kenya or countries in Asia, and they're selling themselves so cheap. And often, the local men leave them in such a sad situation that they have nothing and don't know where to go next.

I have this vision of educating girls before they come here, to prepare them for what may happen and where to go for help if things go wrong. The life that they are aspiring to live in the UK, they can do it in Kenya if they work hard and get qualifications, then they can get jobs. I want to tell them that if they come to the UK, they may make a lot of money, but they're losing a lot in their family and social life. They'll be looked down upon and

Wanjiku graduating with a Master's in Community Development from Bangor University, 2016

discriminated against, and people will call them names. But if they're going to come to the UK, they should be equipped to know what their rights are. Come in as a nurse or a doctor, but don't come through the back door because it's a trap, and you can imagine how difficult it is when you haven't got the right papers to be here.

It's amazing that in the work that I do, I see so many women that are in the situation that I was in, so it's an issue that's very close to my heart. I tell them I've gone through something similar and give them hope. Everybody thinks, how can I survive in this foreign country on my own with the children? So I say to them that at least they've got somebody holding their hand. I also make a point of introducing myself to every BME person that I meet and tell them where my offices are, and invite them for a cup of tea. The people that I'm supporting here are on their own and very isolated. I feel privileged and blessed to be able to help people in this way. I've been in this role now for over fourteen years, and I've really enjoyed it and couldn't ask for a better job.

I thank God and am so grateful for everything I've had in the UK, but this is my children's home, not mine. I left Kenya because I thought life was much better here, and it's not. There may be positive things—we've got a good health system, good roads and good schools. But on the other side, the social life is really bad, and it's much easier to get stressed or depressed here or to have more mental health issues than back home.

Sometimes I wonder what would have happened to me had I gone on with life in Kenya. Where would I be? I made the choice to come here, and nobody forced me. My only regret is that I've lost a lot of time with family and friends and can't spend as much time with them as I would like. In the last few years, I've gotten really homesick for Kenya. I listen to music on Kenyan radio every morning and switch on Kenyan news in the evening. And I started a group from my house called the North Wales Kenyan Community, and we come together every so often and share our food, music, and we talk, discussing anything happening in Kenya. That's one way of elevating homesickness when you have people that are from the same background as yourself.

Wanjiku at a coffee farm in Kenya on a recent visit to see family, 2018

But I'm definitely going back to Kenya when I'm still young and strong and can give something back. I want to give back through charitable work and supporting people. I would definitely do a lot of work with victims of domestic abuse in Kenya.

Overall, I'm a very positive person. It takes me a lot to be negative about something. Because of the confidence I grew up with, that's never left me. But some of the girls I'm supporting now weren't that lucky. Some didn't even have parents growing up, so I really am grateful to my parents, and it's what has helped me fight, and what is now helping me to fight for other people.

# Giving Life

## Vernesta Cyril
**NURSE AND MIDWIFE**

*I've never forgotten my roots, but I never feel that I'm more important than somebody else. I just feel that whoever they are, it doesn't matter what kind of creed or race; I try and support them and give them the confidence to feel they are important too.*

Vernesta as a nurse

I was born in St Lucia and had two sisters and three brothers. I had lots of friends, and we ran around in the rain and skipped rope with a scratchy vine from a mahogany tree. I grew up in a very Christian home and went to a Church of England school, which was one of the best schools around. I loved school and was very good at maths. I was also lucky because my uncle worked for the Education Department, so I got lots of books, which I'd lend to my friends, and we'd sit outside and read. So I had a fair bit of knowledge about the United Kingdom as well as other countries in the world.

I'd always wanted to do midwifery, and in 1962, when I was nineteen, I had an opportunity to come to the UK, as a lot of young people were being recruited from the islands to do nursing. Most of my friends were in London, but my husband, Peter and an aunt were in Newport, so that's where I ended up. Over the years, we had three sons.

I first trained as a nurse, and after a year, decided to do midwifery. When I graduated, I worked at a midwifery hospital for four years until it closed. I then worked at the Royal Gwent Hospital in an independent midwifery unit, where I gained a lot of experience. I was surprised to win the Most Promising Midwife of the Year award in 1973, as all I wanted to do was work to earn money to look after the children and give them a good life.

Balancing work with home life was a challenge. In the summer when the boys were home, I'd do my colleagues' night shifts, so I was home during the day and I'd have the holiday time with them. It was a juggle bringing them up, but mostly they were very good boys. Peter would work shifts as well, so we were always balancing things, making sure the boys had food and clothes. I did a lot of baking, knitting and sewing too. I like a bit of glamour and was always making new dresses with material I'd buy from London. I made my own enjoyment, I think, because otherwise, I think I would have gone mental with what I was facing here, with the discrimination and nonsense going on around me.

Sometimes I had to bulldoze my way in and make people know I was there and to see what I was doing. After eighteen months at my job, I applied for a manager's post and got it, though it wasn't easy. Some of my colleagues were older and had been there a long time and had a problem with me being their boss. I overcame this in the end because I told them that we didn't have to be friends and reminded them that we were working for the benefit of the women we were looking after. Either you stand up to people, or you break down, and I'm sure there are mental health issues with a lot of Black people here because they weren't strong enough to stand up to people.

There was always an element of jealousy and racism, as to why a person didn't get a post, and that we were coming over and taking their jobs. They didn't see that you had to work hard to get where you are. A lot of us took the opportunity to get educated and bettered ourselves in whatever job we were doing. I had to push myself and work hard for what I wanted to accomplish. And I always tried to give my best and do better because a Black person in a position has to work ten times as hard as their white person counterpart, and I think it still happens today. But I think for others it didn't matter and they didn't look at your colour. They looked at your work and how you presented yourself.

So there were a lot of trials and

Vernesta winning UK Midwife of the Year Award, 2006

tribulations, but I think I overcame them. When I got the OBE in 1999, I didn't tell my colleagues—they just found out. But it's the humility in me. I'm not looking to people to say what I got. People have to take me as they find me. For me, the *pièce de résistance* was getting the UK Midwife of the Year award in 2006. That was really an accomplishment. Nowhere in my thoughts did I ever dream of getting such an accolade. I was just doing a job that I loved.

At one stage, the hospital trust asked me to be part of an equality and diversity group they were setting up. Later on, I did a teaching and assessing diploma, as well as social psychology, and was teaching. I was also chair of the Race Equality Council and WEN, a women's organisation in Cardiff because one of the things that I wanted to do was to make a difference. So I got involved in so many things, trying to think how could I help humanity. I was never there just for myself, what I can get out of it. I was always there to see what I could give.

I'm still supporting people in the community, but not on as high a scale as I was being on boards and different things, just the odd bit keeping my brain ticking and supporting younger people because I feel even more so now, a lot of young people need support and guidance, to make them feel proud of themselves. They need confidence in themselves as well because once they get one blip in something, like going for a job and not getting it, things like that just put them down.

So you need to build that confidence up in them to say you are important and don't let anybody else make you feel that you're not. Whatever you want, you can do it. But it's important to focus on what you want to do and not to deviate from that focus, and to be bold, brave and strong. You'll come against stumbling blocks, but you have to fight to get over these rocks. And that was my motto. I didn't let people keep me down. I was like a tennis ball. When you bounce me down, then I come up again. I won't stay down.

Vernesta receiving an OBE for her services in the community, 1999

I still think there are people who are not very nice and use racist connotations. But there are people who are genuine and like you for who you are, so you have to differentiate at times. But I think when you have a good education, and you've got a strong family behind you, then you carry that along with you. My aunts and my mum were very strong women and gave me good advice.

My dream was to go back to St Lucia and work as a midwife. It didn't happen because I got settled here with a family, and things were not the same as when I left. But I joined the Black and Caribbean Association in London and went to the carnival there every year with a big group of friends and sometimes took the boys. It was very important to me to have somewhere I could go to get the good vibes of the Caribbean. I've never forgotten my roots, but I never feel that I'm more important than somebody else. I just feel that whoever they are, it doesn't matter what kind of creed or race; I try and support them. When I look back, I think I may have made changes to some people's lives, giving them confidence and making them feel they are important too.

# Gifts of Learning

## Grace Kerry
**EDUCATION CONSULTANT AND AUTHOR, FOUNDER AND EXECUTIVE DIRECTOR OF GIFT OF GRACE EDUCATION PROJECT**

*My mother's love and teaching are always with me. She taught me to always stand up for what I believe in, and I would advise anyone facing challenges in life, to just be strong and believe in themselves.*

Grace, age 6, in her new Brownie uniform, with her parents on the grounds of her father's church in Lagos.

I was born in a small town called Nsukka, in Eastern Nigeria. My father was a clergyman in the Anglican Church, eventually rising to the status of venerable archdeacon of Asaba Diocese, Delta State. My father was sent regularly to different rural villages to start a new school or church, so when I was growing up, we moved every year or two. We weren't rich, but we were happy, with a love that made everything beautiful. My mother was a trailblazer for women in politics, in the church and socially. In the early 1960s, she was elected as the first female senator and parliamentarian in the first Republic of Nigeria. I covered her inspirational biography in my book entitled, *The Senator: A Remarkable Story*.

I had three brothers, two older and one younger than me, but my second brother passed away in an accident, aged five. I attended a secondary school in Port Harcourt, Eastern Nigeria, run partly by white missionaries. It was a huge privilege for me because growing up, not many parents could afford to pay for their children's secondary school education, but my parents, particularly my mother, were very determined that I attend school to the level I was capable of.

When I left secondary school, my parents were determined that I go to the UK to further my education. After a couple of years, I arrived in 1961 to study nursing at

Joyce Green Hospital in Kent, but due to overwhelming homesickness, I left. I missed my loving and close-knit family in Nigeria and found the environment not very friendly, mostly due to differences in lifestyle and culture. When I eventually left nursing, I enrolled to study advanced English at the then Regent Street Polytechnic in London.

Grace at her PhD graduation, University of Wales, Cardiff, 1985

I got married in London shortly thereafter. My husband, Nduka Okoh, and I moved to Glasgow in 1962, where we lived for ten years and had four children. We returned to Nigeria in 1972 and I studied for my first degree in English language and literature at Ahmadu Bello University in Zaria, where my husband was a lecturer. He lived and worked mostly in Nigeria, where he rose from a lecturer to a professor of education and until he retired, was vice-chancellor of the University of Benin City, Nigeria.

Meanwhile, I returned to the UK in 1978 to do my Master's Degree in educational psychology and came back again in 1982 to study for a doctorate degree at the University of Wales, Cardiff. My subject of choice was special educational needs in primary and secondary schools. I finished in 1985 with Commendation.

It was difficult to find meaningful work for two or three years after my studies, but between 1989 to 1992, I had a job as a peripatetic tutor at the Multicultural Education Centre (MEC) in Bristol. In 1991, I also got a job as a lecturer at the Open University in Wales, teaching a course called 'Race, Education and Society', which I taught until 1999.

From 1992 to 1997, I was a primary and secondary school advisory teacher in Gwent, as well as a member of the Gwent County Inspection team, based in Gilwern, near Abergavenny. I was working so hard for my family and caring for my elderly mother. Between 1993 and 1995, I accepted a part-time post as a visiting lecturer in educational psychology at Gwent College of Higher Education in Newport. As an advisory teacher, I also trained

Grace receiving a certificate as an Ambassador for Peace from the Universal Peace Federation, 2012

foreign-language speaking assistants who worked with teachers in Gwent to support ethnic minority children in primary schools. I believe this was the start of the support being offered to BAME school children in Wales.

When work ended in Gwent, I got a job for a year in 1998 as acting head of the special needs department of St Teilos Church in Wales Secondary School in Cardiff. This was followed by a position at the Parade Language Centre in Cardiff, teaching English as a second language from 1999 to 2003. I later moved on to teach English at MENFA Charity Centre in Grangetown in Cardiff, between 2004 to 2010. I regularly worked as a supply teacher in secondary schools in Gwent and Cardiff whenever possible. It was in my workplaces that I encountered one of my greatest challenges, which was racism, but which I managed to overcome in order to get on and to be able to care for my children.

In 2012, I was inspired and motivated to set up a charity

Opening day, Isienu Primary School, Owerre-Olubor, April 2013, with pupils wearing the original Gift of Grace T-shirts and waving Welsh and Nigerian flags. Grace (*back, fourth from the left*) with some of the school's patrons, teachers and supporters

for vulnerable children in Nigeria called the 'Gift of Grace Education Project' (Gift of Grace for short). My mother and I talked a lot about building a primary school for rural children because, for decades, the state school system in Nigeria has been failing our children. Primary school classes in rural schools are overcrowded and in a pathetic state, while the teachers are poorly trained, unmotivated and often not paid their meagre salaries for months, and apathy sets in. So, education in rural primary schools is failing.

After my mother passed away and I retired, I decided to put our dream into action, so I started an educational charity in my father's place of birth for 120 poor and vulnerable children, mainly girls aged five to twelve. I set up the charity in 2012, and the following year opened the

Gift of Grace Education Project pupils inside the church hall, expressing their joy, with Grace (*in blue*) and some of the teachers standing behind them, 2017

Saturday school, where our pupils are offered supplementary education and food.

Gift of Grace is constantly fundraising to keep our charity going. This school is my main goal and focus at the moment, and raising money to sustain it is vital for our future. Souter Trust has regularly supported us with funding, as has the Welsh Government too. At the moment, all the classes are taught in a hired church hall, but our end goal is to raise enough funds to build five to six classroom blocks and probably a teachers' house to make the school our special dream place.

There are many things I've achieved in life, but my two main passions are educating children, especially girls, because of the importance of education in our lives. As the philosopher Epictetus said, 'Only the educated are free.' My other main passion is feeding poor children because, as the saying goes, 'health is wealth.'

My mother's love and teaching are always with me. She taught me to always stand up for what I believe in, and I would advise anyone facing challenges in life, to just be strong and believe in themselves.

# Joyful Harmony

## Sunita Menon
**PROFESSIONAL SINGER**

*For me, music is the best way of connecting cultures. It's something everybody can relate to and is the easiest medium for bringing people together.*

I was born in the state of Kerala, India. My father was an army officer, and every three years, he was transferred, so the first half of my childhood was quite nomadic, and we moved all over to places like Delhi and Bombay. When I was in Year 7, my father retired from the army and took a job in Kerala, and we settled in Cochin, where I remained until I graduated.

From the time I was a child, I'd always wanted to be a singer, and I can't remember wanting to be anything else. I grew up listening to my mum sing in Hindi, so suppose I inherited my talent from my mother and interest from my father, who wanted me to learn Carnatic classical music.

Kerala is one of the most happening states in India when it comes to arts and culture, and I had a fantastic time doing music when I was growing up, and I don't remember too many weeks when I was not competing in musical youth festivals, each with over 500 competitors. Later on, I represented my university at the national level on three occasions.

While the Carnatic tradition was my initial introduction to music, in college, I got introduced to Western music, and

Sunita with the band, 13AD

158  SEVENTY YEARS OF STRUGGLE AND ACHIEVEMENT

after I graduated, I joined one of India's biggest rock bands, called 13AD. I was their lead female vocalist for about four and a half years and toured the length and breadth of India with them and abroad, which was a really fascinating journey.

Before I got married, I tried to do a stint in a courier company called DHL. I worked there for about a year, and I hated every minute of it. I realised I'm not cut out for a 9–5 job, as I like to be doing different things every day. Along with singing, I love painting and cooking and doing creative things around the house, which all excite me, and a mundane job would have killed me.

Sunita, (*back, third from left*), an EMWWAA Arts and Culture award recipient, 2013

I came to Wales after I got married to my husband, Sudhir, who was working here. I've only ever lived in Wales, but it's been brilliant, and the people have been so nice to me here. But for my first six years, I did absolutely no singing, as I didn't have any contacts. Then, a GP in Wales got to know from somebody that I'm classically trained, and she wanted to take some lessons from me. She also wanted to learn Hindi songs, and in time, she introduced me to her core group of friends, who asked her to organise a show for me. So I have to give it to her for introducing me to music again after a great break.

My first show in Wales was for 250 people. Here, that's considered massive, whereas in India, I'm used to performing for 5,000 people, which is still not considered a huge crowd, so it's taken me some time to get used to the Welsh concept of huge numbers. There's much more happening in places like the Midlands, and the Welsh music scene is a bit too quiet for my liking. It's a lot different and better now than when I first came, but I still feel we can do more. But I'm grateful for the wonderful platform that WAWAA has given me as a way for people to come to know me.

Most of the time, I perform here, but there's only so much I can do in this country. So during the summer, and the Easter and Christmas holidays, I go to India to perform. I'm known in the Bollywood industry in India, so my musicians there always try to encourage me to stay. But I have commitments in

Wales, especially my two beautiful girls, who are my priority. After I've seen them into university, I'll have a lot more time on my hands to pursue my interests. And for me, I don't feel age is a factor. Age is just a number, and my whole life is there for me.

My older daughter is an extremely passionate dancer, and there's music in both of them in some form or the other, which I'm really happy about. So I tell my kids and anybody I meet to follow your passion with conviction and believe that it will happen. There's no way it won't happen because, especially with my journey, I faced only obstacles when I was growing up.

My entire family are professionals, like my brother and cousins are orthopaedic surgeons, and I'm the only artist in the family, so although my father really pushed me to learn music, he still wanted me to be a professional with an interest in music rather than a musician. On top of that, I come from a very conservative family, so when I went into a rock band, it sent shockwaves throughout the entire family, and it was very hard. My father didn't talk to me for about a year and a half. But then later on, when he started seeing me perform and the kind of musicians who were giving me respect and honouring me, then he really changed and was very proud of me.

I love singing and only sing what I want to and what gives me joy. One of my strengths is that I can sing in about sixteen or seventeen languages. When I'm doing shows for Banglas or a group from Tamnar or Gujarat, I've been able to give them what they want to listen to, and if I have a Western crowd, I will sing purely Western music.

I used to perform at a regatta in Kerala for the Indian Naval Academy, which is the largest military academy in Asia. Every year they'd invite thirteen or fourteen countries to compete, so if there were Brazilians, I'd do a Portuguese number and an Arabic number for Arab countries and a Baila for Sri Lankans, so they were all happy. For me, music is the best way of connecting cultures. It's something everybody can relate to and is the easiest medium for bringing people together.

# Forging one's path

# The Culture of Creativity

## Leanne Rahman
**FREELANCE ARTS CONSULTANT**

*A lot of my journey feels like it was by accident, but you have to grab an opportunity when it comes across your path. If it's your burning desire to do something, then don't let anybody tell you that you can't. It's going to be tough, but you've got to put your boxing gloves on and just go for it.*

Leanne, age 3, with her grandfather, 'Pa Trot' in Barbados, 1978

I was born in Barbados in 1975 and lived there until I was nine. My dad is from Barbados, and my mum is from Cardiff, though much of her family were originally from the Caribbean. As a child, I was a bit of a water baby and a good swimmer. Every day before and after school, I swam in the sea, and I told everyone I was going to be an Olympic swimmer. I also wanted to be a vet, as I loved animals. I used to rescue lots of injured animals from the beach and bring them home to nurse them back to health.

As I grew, my parents' relationship began to break down, and shortly after my ninth birthday, my sisters and I left Barbados with my mum to live with my grandparents in Wales. I didn't want to leave my dad or Barbados, but I was excited to come to the UK. We didn't have any warm clothes, as they're expensive to buy in the Caribbean, and when we arrived in November, the cold literally pierced our bones. Everything looked so grey in comparison to the Caribbean, where everything is so bright and vibrant, so I just thought, my God, there's no colour here. It took a while for me to get used to it.

That winter was also the first time my sisters and I had ever seen snow. One morning, after there had been a heavy snowfall overnight, we bounded through the door barefoot and in our pyjamas and threw ourselves into the snow. We were covered like snow angels, laughing and screaming like fools. It took us about ten minutes to realise that snow actually makes you cold and wet, so we stood there sopping wet and shivering, but we just had to experience it to the fullest.

It's strange when you first come to a new place and have to interact with new people. Understanding the lingo had me upside down for a long time, and it took me what felt like an eternity to understand what anybody was saying. But my Caribbean accent disappeared pretty quickly within a couple of months, and I now feel that I speak 100 per cent like I'm from Cardiff.

I went to Mount Stuart Primary School in the Docks and was the pupil that was always half an hour late to school in the mornings, strolling in on Caribbean time. But it was amazing to go to a school that was so diverse, particularly compared to the lack of diversity I experienced in Barbados. Attending Mount Stuart was a very special experience, especially due to the headmistress, the late Mrs Betty Campbell MBE, who made all pupils feel welcome and valuable, regardless of their backgrounds or where they came from.

My mum raised me and my sisters as a single parent and worked extremely hard, holding down as many jobs as she could. During holiday periods, she couldn't really be there to look after us, so we tried to enrol in as many summer schemes as possible. One of these was a filmmaking workshop for local youngsters run by the Black Film and Video Workshop in Wales, and I also volunteered for Butetown Carnival, delivering Caribbean dance workshops in schools. This is where my interest in the arts began, as I was inspired by the wealth of creativity within the local community.

Things weren't as easy as they could have been, being female and from Butetown as well, where many young people have experienced this postcode being used against them. I was also quite young when I had my first child, which added another layer of difficulty and struggle. I was almost nine months' pregnant, sitting my A-level exams, and just managed to pass by the skin of my teeth. I remember a few of the teachers being really negative towards me, expecting and even advising me to drop out of school. I wouldn't advise anyone to have a baby while studying because it's really tough going mentally and physically, but if you've got a strong focus, determination and a good support network around you, you can achieve, no matter what.

After my son was born, I took a year out and then enrolled at Cardiff Met (then UWIC) and studied art and design. I carried out my work experience at BBC Wales and also with Red Flannel Films, a women's filmmaking company that focused on women's issues. After college, I got one of the last places in film school at UWCN's Caerleon campus (now the University of South Wales). I was the first member of my family to attend university.

On graduating, I volunteered for the International Black Film Festival, Wales, for five years. Then I undertook various administrative jobs for local charities, who were doing great work, but I got to a point where I wanted to do something I felt was more meaningful. I got a position at Minority Ethnic Women's Network, which was my first role as a support worker. The job entailed promoting access to green space for ethnic minority women and children in order to improve their health and wellbeing. It was a great role and really rewarding to see how the voluntary sector operated and how you could make a difference to people's lives.

After a couple of years, I was approached by the Black Voluntary Sector Network (BVSNW) regarding an opening for a women's arts development officer. The role aimed to increase the number of the agency's female artists across Wales, particularly outside of Cardiff. It was an amazing opportunity for me, especially to do something hands-on once again within the creative industries.

During my time at BVSNW, I travelled a lot, meeting artists throughout Wales and identifying what the barriers were to them finding work and whether they felt that they faced any discrimination or prejudice when trying to gain employment. This information was fed back to the Arts Council of Wales, which aimed to increase fair and equitable opportunities for artists and creative professionals of colour.

We made some progress and some small steps forward. It was a huge amount of work for a very small team, but I really enjoyed it and was passionate about the work. Some of the artists I met were truly inspirational, and I worked on some fantastic community arts festivals and projects, helping to preserve cultural traditions while raising awareness among wider communities in Wales. It was heart-breaking when BVSNW closed around 2015. I was out of work for a time and decided to volunteer with Butetown History and Arts Centre. I also joined Voluntary Arts as an advisory panel member for Wales and worked on Tiger Bay Presents, a fringe festival at the Wales Millennium Centre.

Black History Month Wales is by far the largest and longest programme I was involved in over the past twelve years. The first event I co-organised with Nicky Delgado took place at Butetown Youth Club, and while it was small and a bit rough around the edges, it exceeded our expectations, and our local communities valued it. We were

Leanne working at BVSNW, c.2011

then asked to expand to include African diaspora people from other parts of Wales, enabling them to experience their cultural heritage and traditions. We also worked with teachers to create curriculum-linked programmes that could be run in schools. I'm less involved with this work now, but it's amazing to see the vital legacy that's grown from such small beginnings.

Education is for life, and having good teachers is something I feel very passionate about. If you keep bombarding young people with negativity, especially those from BAME and less affluent communities, continuously telling them that they're not good enough or are not going to achieve, it's so soul-destroying and damaging to their development, as they grow up believing it. It makes me angry and upset, so I feel very fortunate that in some of the positions I've found myself in, I've been able to help young people.

I believe that knowledge and opportunities are for sharing. I've always been enthused by seeing people achieve their goals, maybe set up their own business, develop as a practising artist or just do whatever they aspire to do. The journey is very often not in a straight line, and a lot of mine feels like it was by accident, but you have to grab an opportunity when it comes across your path. We have to teach young people not to shy away from difficult things and not be too rigid in what they think the future holds for them. We all need to have more open minds in how we view achievement, failure and success. It's in our nature to doubt ourselves and our abilities, but if it's your burning desire to do something, then don't let anybody tell

Leanne on her wedding day in Barbados, walked down the 'aisle' by her mother, Geraldine, Valentine's Day, 2002

Leanne on her first family holiday to Cuba with husband, Rhys and children, Leroy, Jyrell and Naomi, 2006

you that you can't. Only you can stop yourself from achieving your dream. It's going to be tough, but you've got to put on your boxing gloves and just go for it.

My grandfather was an amazing role model in my life. He stowed away on a ship from St Lucia when he was thirteen and ended his journey in Tiger Bay. He stayed and married a Welsh lady, and they were married for 70 years before they passed away. I'd love to have the special kind of relationship that my nan and gramps had. My mum has also been a massive inspiration to me and is my rock. I don't think I would have been able to achieve half of what I've done in my life without somebody like her by my side. She's had to overcome many hurdles, coming back from the Caribbean alone with three young children and starting life all over again. She's always been so positive and active in the community and has instilled in me determination, courage and strength. I've also been really fortunate to have met such a good, loving and supportive man in my husband. We've been together for nearly 30 years now, and we have three wonderful children and one beautiful granddaughter.

I think every person needs strong personalities in their lives, the kind of characters that can really make a massive difference and help mould and support you. And if you're unable to find that kind of role model close to home, we have to be able to provide a place where youngsters can get that kind of inspiration from, like at school or a local youth club. Meeting wonderful people along your journey opens your eyes to possibilities and endless opportunities, while you can also make friends, mentors and confidants on your way through life. I'm very fortunate to have been able to meet people who feel so passionately about community, culture and creativity, and who have enriched my life forever.

I was surprised to be nominated for an EMWWAA award in 2017 and to win in the category of Arts, Culture and

Leanne receiving her EMWWAA award from former First Minister of Wales, Rhodri Morgan, 2017.

Sports. Recognition for my work has never entered my mind whatsoever. For me, it's always been about doing something in my community and in the arts that I love. I always prefer to be in the background, working hard to make things happen, as a convener to create opportunities for communities to access quality cultural activities and events.

A dream of mine would be to, one day, run my own arts centre. I feel we have lost quite a lot in the local community in terms of places where people can come together, express themselves creatively, eat good food and share stories. I could see myself being very happy and comfortable in a creative space just like this. Maybe in the future, I can make it happen.

# Vocalising Strength

## Humie Webbe
**STRATEGIC EQUALITY AND DIVERSITY LEAD, NATIONAL TRAINING FEDERATION FOR WALES**

*Sometimes we have to find an inner strength and elevate ourselves, but in a way that we're proud of everybody's achievements.*

I was born in Cardiff, the eldest of my siblings born in Wales, along with my twin sister, Sondra. I also have two older sisters, on my father's side, who were born in St Kitts. My oldest sister, Bernadette, was raised by her maternal grandmother and aunt after her mother died in childbirth. My father and Bernadette's mother were childhood sweethearts and were both seventeen. He sent for Bernadette when she was nine years old and she lived in London. Four years later, my father had another child, Paulette. He came to the UK in 1954 to make a life for himself and his new family, but Paulette's mother didn't want to leave St Kitts. He then met and married my mother in the UK.

There were six of us at home, so we were a noisy family, but growing up, everybody had a big family. My mother and father were very family-oriented, so we saw our cousins regularly. We lived in an area called Ely, and there were about four or five other Black families who would all go to each other's houses and have parties. So, growing up, I was very much aware of my Caribbean roots and was steeped in Caribbean culture.

My father worked for a time in the steelworks. He was a very gregarious, social animal and had a big allotment in the garden, where he would grow vegetables. I wouldn't say we were poor, but everything had to be shared. My mother was always very careful in how she managed the household and made sure we all had chores. She could put her hand to anything. She made our clothes, knitted, crocheted, embroidered and pretty much everything. She schooled us in how to do all of these things too, but because I'm the only person in the family who's left-handed, it used to take me ages to learn all of them.

My life was a mixture of doing chores and going to school, as well as Sunday school—sometimes three times

Twin sisters, Sondra and Humie, age 7

on a Sunday, and no television on Sundays until late afternoon, just gospel songs. My mother was a Seventh Day Adventist, and we went to church on Saturday as well.

I loved music and was fortunate that I went to a school where the headteacher had a Bachelor of Arts in music and had a really good approach to learning. He could play seven different instruments and would teach anyone that wanted to learn. We also sang choral songs in assembly.

I started singing with my sisters when I was very young, and my sister, Sondra and I won a church *Eisteddfod* competition when we were seven. Then we formed an acapella choir with our younger sister, Jacqueline, and I used to do the vocal arrangements. We would go round the Methodist churches singing songs with our three-part harmonies. People used to be fascinated by these little children, so the Webbe sisters became famous locally on the Methodist church circuit. My twin, Sondra, and I used to also play violin and recorder and were in the choir and orchestra and did all these sorts of wonderful things.

As I got older, from around the age of fifteen, I had more responsibility for cooking and running the household. My parents had got divorced, and my mother, at the age of 42, trained to be a nurse. After qualifying, she chose to work night shifts, in time, becoming a senior night nurse, so I helped around the house while she slept during the day. I always grew up thinking I could do whatever I wanted to do, and nobody could tell me otherwise. As I enjoyed cooking, I made the decision to study catering at Barry College of Further Education and became our class representative. So began my interest in trying to make a difference for others.

After I graduated, at the age of eighteen, I went with my father to the Caribbean for six weeks. That's when I found my culture and heritage, and it was my first time living in an environment where Black people were the majority and in positions of power and influence. I was also struck by how ambitious people were for themselves, their families and their country. There is no university in St Kitts, so to advance their careers, people had to leave home and go to another country. My thinking about what I wanted to do with my life totally changed by the time I came back to the UK. I realised that up to that point, I was taking education and opportunities for granted, and rather than just having a job, I wanted to have a career that made a difference to people.

I started working for the South Glamorgan Health Authority and was employed in catering at Hamadryad Hospital and then at Ely Hospital. During this time, I was asked to join a band made up of a family who was related to us by marriage. Later, my sisters, Jacky and Veronica, joined the band and I became the lead singer and songwriter. We used to sing at festivals and in clubs, and I'd often go straight from a gig to work at the hospital. I stayed at Ely Hospital for nine years until I became pregnant and then decided that catering was no longer for me and I was going to retrain.

I had my son, Saul, at age 29 and had split up with his father. My son was diagnosed on the autism spectrum when he was about nine, but he'd been seeing a child psychologist and speech therapist from the age of three. Having Saul changed the way in which I sought employment, and I worked freelance for a number of years. When I went into the voluntary sector, they were always very supportive. If I didn't have anybody to look after Saul, I brought him with me, and he sat in the pushchair.

One of my first jobs, after my son was born, was working part-time for a local residents' association and as a clerk for the governing body of a school in the Vale of Glamorgan. This led me to work in the third and public sectors. My various roles have included director of a history project, project officer with the National Museum Wales, a national diversity role with Mind Cymru and operational manager for the Cardiff Communities First programme.

Through my interest in music and the arts, I began to work more with young people and managed to find employment in youth and community work, while I studied for my BA Honours degree in Community Education on a part-time basis. I progressed to managerial roles and studied full time for my Master's in Project Management.

I have also worked as a freelance consultant for heritage organisations, raising funds for arts and cultural projects. My background in music education and youth and community work enabled me to develop several school-based projects and choirs. I also organised music residentials, festivals and carnivals, and ran an after-school provision for young people with high-functioning autism.

I've often been drawn to projects to do with disabled people, women, BME groups, and anything where you're at a disadvantage because that's my background, and not everybody can advocate for themselves.

I have been fortunate to work with so many inspirational people who have supported me in my career and shown me how to build resilience and campaign for things you believe in. Two of my proudest achievements have been working with the Welsh education icon, Betty Campbell, to establish

Jacky, Patti and Humie at the Bay Divas Christmas show, St David's Hall, 2012

the Butetown Community Choir, which incorporated the all-female United Harmony Singers and the Butetown Junior Schools Choir. During my ten-year tenure, the choirs sang for people like Paul Robeson Jr and HRH Prince Philip, Duke of Edinburgh. As well, with my dear friend and original Bay diva, Patti Flynn, I established the Butetown Bay Jazz Heritage Festival to recognise and celebrate the musical heritage of the Cardiff Docklands area.

I'm now employed by the National Training Federation for Wales in the work-based learning (WBL) sector working in partnership with colleges, training providers, and employers, providing opportunities for individuals to have structured learning in the workplace. An example of this would be apprenticeships, where students get paid to obtain on-the-job experience and industry-specific qualifications, such as those in engineering or childcare.

My role is also to support WBL providers to develop strategies and approaches to increase the diversity of apprenticeship learners, in particular, disabled people and individuals from Black, Asian and minority ethnic (BAME) communities, while also striving to achieve a greater gender balance across sectors that are traditionally dominated by males or females.

I'm one of the few people of colour in a sort of decision-making strategic-level post. Often when I'm in the minority, even if I've got nothing to say, I try to make my presence felt because I'm conscious that I'm trying to pave the way for the next person because we don't get those opportunities. I think a lot of it is to do with the perception people from the Caribbean or Black and Asian communities

Humie performing at the Butetown Bay Jazz Heritage Festival, 2010

have about themselves being worthy enough to go into certain positions. When people ask me how I got my jobs, I just tell them I looked at the application and applied, and at interviews, I think I've got nothing to lose.

I would like to carry on in my current role, as it allows me

Humie and her father outside Westminster Abbey for St Kitts Independence Day, 2015

to work closely with the Welsh Government in policy areas of equality, diversity and inclusion (EDI). My aim is to ensure that all forms of discrimination are eliminated, particularly in educational institutions, employment, and health and social care.

In the past 10 years, I have worked more in the equality, diversity and inclusion arena. I was the national diversity coordinator for the Time to Change Wales mental health anti-stigma campaign and was instrumental in increasing the participation of BAME communities in the campaign and supporting them to deliver mental health anti-stigma projects.

As the main carer for an adult autistic son and for my father, who recently passed away after losing his battle with Alzheimer's, I have campaigned for better health and social care services that are culturally appropriate. I have held national advisory roles with the Arts Council, Creative and Cultural Skills sector, and am currently co-chair of the Learning Disability Ministerial Advisory group. I am also a member of the BAME group set up by the Welsh Education Minister, exploring how to include diverse histories in the Welsh curriculum.

After thirty-odd years working in the public and private sector, I find that whatever job I have, I shape it to what I want it to be. And it's lovely to be recognised, and I do appreciate everything

Humie receiving an EMWWAA Rhodri Morgan award from Welsh First Minister Mark Drakeford, 2019

that people have said about me and given to me, but there is valour in people just doing what they've been doing. Sometimes, we have to find that inner strength and elevate ourselves because nobody's going to be elevating us; but we have to elevate ourselves in a way that we're proud of everybody's achievements.

# Music from the Heart

## Banani Sinha Ray
**INDIAN CLASSICAL MUSIC SINGER AND PERFORMER**

*When we learn music, we not only learn music. We learn a lot of things like how to believe.*

I was born in Calcutta, India. I grew up in my grandfather's house in a village, together with my uncle's family. I'm the second of four children, and my uncle had five, so there were nine children growing up together in a big house, which we called 'Jora Bari'. We had a lovely time in childhood, and they were golden days for me, with open airfields and lots of gardens of flowers and fruits. In the summertime, we used to go swimming in the ponds.

My father was a doctor and always wanted me to be a doctor too, the way all Indian people want their children to follow in their paths. My mother was a housewife, but before she got married, she had been a singer and radio performer too. Growing up, there was always pressure for me to get married to a good husband, but my mother wanted me to be a singer and to be famous. Maybe she put her dream onto me, so I think I am what I am today with my mother's blessing and pushing.

I was born into a very musical family, and everyone used to sing or play instruments. My father could play flute and tabla. My grandfather used to sing and play the harmonium. One of my uncles was a renowned musician and tabla player. He and another uncle, who played sitar, both attained the honorific title of Pandit for their talents. Another uncle was a classical vocalist and disciple of Pandit Narayan Rao Joshi, who used to come and stay for a month with us. In the summers, Kathak dancers from Banaras also used to come and perform, and I'd listen to them all the time, which is how my musical journey started.

So, from my childhood, I was deeply immersed in music and always thrived to excel in the Indian classical style. My mother started teaching me to sing when I was six. Later, I trained in Kirana Gharana music, under the tutelage of a maestro, my guru, Pandit Biswanath Ghosh, who was a disciple of Ustad Amir Khan. I also trained with Manindra

Musical Banani, age 21

Chandra Day and my uncle, Pandit Soroj Ray, who was a disciple of Ustad Keramatulla Khan, who taught me rhythm and was my mentor too. I used to go to different events with him to perform and am one of the winners of the 1979 All Bengal Competition in the Kayhal category.

I then conferred Sangit Probhakar and Sangit Bisharad music diplomas from the University of Allahabad and Chandigarh University, and having done science in school, I went for a BSc at the University of Calcutta. I began an MSc, which I later completed, and at the same time, my uncle put me in Rabindra Bharati University in Calcutta for an MA in music. When I was in Calcutta, I worked as a biology teacher for a while.

Then I got married through an arranged marriage and came to the UK, first to Derby, in the springtime, with all of the flowers, which I love. I was newly married and happy at the time. I had brought over my tanpura, a stringed instrument, but had always wanted to learn piano. So I learned for a few years and did up to Grade 5. My husband was a young doctor and quite busy and had to move around for training, so we moved to Wrexham, north Wales. My two sons were born in north Wales, and my brother came over, so we stayed there for a few years, but it was frustrating for me because there was no Indian culture there. I practised my music, but I had been performing and learning all the time in Calcutta, and I thought we would be going back.

It wasn't so easy to go home because I was busy with the children, so I decided when I was in the UK, I'd give my children everything, so they could grow up nicely. But after ten years, I went back to India and stayed there for five years. My husband also came over for a few years, and my boys went to Calcutta International School.

The school had a British curriculum, but we later discovered that Calcutta University wouldn't accept this, so after A levels, the boys wouldn't have been able to pursue a professional career. So we decided it would be better for

Banani playing tanpura at a Poetry and Esraj event in Birmingham, 2017

their education if we returned to the UK. We went first to north Wales and eventually settled in Cardiff. I did a three-year degree course in computers and started to work for the NHS, but my mind was always on music. The whole office knew I was keen on music, and they all supported and encouraged me, as they've done until today.

Bangladeshi and Indian people are quite interested in music, so I started teaching their children and adults as well. At one time, I had 25 pupils, but I thought it was too much, and my family was being neglected. Also, teaching can wreck your voice, so I cut it down. I still have twelve or thirteen pupils, and sometimes they disappear and come back again. Some of them are very good and very talented. There's one autistic Bengali boy. When I first met him, he would just listen to me and copy, but now he can read notes. His mum got him a harmonium, and the next time I saw him, he was playing that. His main interest is bonding with the music and singing in Bengali, Hindi and Urdu.

I always think about young people, that if they learn and it's gone to their heart, they can carry on our heritage and culture. When we learn music, we learn not only music. We learn a lot of things like how to believe. I think if children want to do something, they should go for it and be frank with their parents that they want to do this. In our time, it was difficult. Now, parents understand, and I notice if a child wants to do singing or play an instrument, parents arrange for their special training. Nowadays, there are lots of opportunities and competitions, and things are more open in the world, so if someone wants to do something, they should just carry on.

Some people from other communities or religions objected to some of the devotional songs, and I felt some threat for the first time after twenty years of being in Cardiff. Most of the songs in our Hindustani classical repertoire have names like Krishna or Shiva, so if you want

Banani performing as a guest artist at the Hall of Fame, Calcutta Club, India, 2018

to learn, you have to use those names. Now I always ask if people are okay with that, and most people don't mind. I don't have a problem with any religions' songs and prayers—to me, it's all the same thing.

Now, I have my own group called Aurav Disha MW, which means, 'a direction of peaceful echo of multicultural Wales'. People have joined our group from all different communities, and our aims are to promote multicultural music and art, especially of young and local artists, and to provide a platform for diverse communities to perform together.

Our group has performed in several places in Cardiff, Bristol and London, and we hope there will be more opportunities in future. In 2019, we performed at an opening ceremony at the National Museum of Cardiff, alongside professional musicians from India, London and locally. I've also been performing quite a lot in places like Birmingham, Reading, Leicester, Bolton and Liverpool. In 2010, I performed at the Ananda Utsav Bengali and Indian Festival in London's Alexandra Palace, where 6,000 people came. Over the three-day festival, there were top-class artists from all over India and Bangladesh, and I represented Wales.

I've also released various DVD albums—*Bangla Melody* in 2010, followed by *AlorKhoje* in 2012, which featured a song I composed myself. *Anurager Rang,* released in 2014, was an album of melody songs, and in 2016, I put out *Chand Herichhe*, with the legendary singer, Saikat Mitra. At the moment, I am working on another Hindi video album, and all of my album songs are telecast regularly on different TV channels in Calcutta. India is still very close to me, and I go every three to four months to Calcutta and do performances in different places, like the Calcutta Club and the Birla Academy of Art and Culture, as well as live television programmes.

Banani recording the *Chand Herichhe* album, 2016

In Cardiff, I've been invited to present and perform at the Central Library on several occasions, which has given me opportunities to interact with Welsh people sharing mutual cultural interests and to increase the awareness of Indian classical music. One of these programmes entitled, 'Vive—One City, Many Cultures' had African, Chinese, Bangladeshi, Pakistani and Indian performers.

The author, Bruce Cardwell, also featured me in his photographic book, *Noteworthy*, about Welsh music, and in 2013, I won a WAWWA award for Arts and Culture, which

was a surprise. As an artist, I work from my heart. I'm really introverted and don't express myself to the public.

Wherever I'm going through life, I just go forward. I've had regrets, but I've got a good family and have always been supported by my husband. Both my children are doctors now. My elder son is a respiratory consultant at Imperial College, and the younger son is doing research on liver transplantation and the Hepatitis B vaccine at Addenbrookes Hospital, Cambridge University. He is also a very good painter and has done several exhibitions and has his own studio in London. They're both very gentle and both love me very much, so at least in this way, I'm a winner.

# The Challenge of Equality

## Aliya Mohammed
**CHIEF EXECUTIVE OFFICER, RACE EQUALITY FIRST**

*If you enjoy your job, it will motivate you, make you learn faster, and you'll naturally want to do it well, which will help you to succeed in any role.*

I was born in Leeds, West Yorkshire. My parents were both from the Punjab, very close to Lahore, Pakistan. As a trader, my great-grandfather first came to the UK in 1890. He and my grandfather lived and worked here more regularly from around 1925, going back regularly to India (what later became Pakistan) to spend large periods of time with their families. During the 1950s, my grandfather returned to Britain to assist the UK Government with labour shortages in the steel, textile and engineering industries. He would bring labourers over in steamships and help get them housed in London. My parents joined their parents in the UK as teenagers in the early 1960s and completed their education, and got married here.

I grew up with lots of relatives within a close-knit family, and it was quite a happy and healthy environment to be brought up in. I'm the middle child of five siblings, and it was a lovely household because there was a lot of noise and a lot of things going on all the time. My parents were clothing manufacturers, supplying large stores, as well as importing and exporting clothes. They also owned a factory and a warehouse, and we used to play in these premises as children. There were trolleys where they'd throw the used material, and we'd jump in and push each other around, so it was a very colourful and enjoyable childhood, both at home and at my parents' workplace too.

I don't have good memories of school, though, and I didn't like the rigid formality, maybe because I was a bit mischievous and didn't like rules. It was also not a very nice environment, and as an adult, I now know that what other BME students and I experienced from some of the teachers and fellow students was racist behaviour which, at times, was quite vicious. I still find it very upsetting to think about, though it happened so many years ago, as it really damaged my confidence. With A levels, I had to take school

Aliya's niece's wedding, with Aliya second from the right, Birmingham, 2015

and really pushed me to gain some experience before I graduated, so while at university, I worked at BBC Television every summer, as well as at various magazines and radio stations. At the BBC, I would mainly shadow a journalist covering a news item, but they'd also give me lots of opportunities to cover stories for myself. One of these was about people with visual impairment who were given the opportunity to learn to fly a plane through voice and navigation control, which was quite an experience in itself.

a bit more seriously because it was something that was going to shape the rest of my life, and I enjoyed this stage a lot more than primary and middle school.

Just before I graduated, I got married to my husband, Ashfaq, so I kind of did things backwards, but I was quite a rebel then. Perhaps I shouldn't have got married at that age, and my parents didn't want me to either. But I really believe that sometimes the wrong decisions bring you to the right places, and that's how I also feel now. I'm still very happily married after 26 years, and we have two grown-up children I'm really proud of, so I certainly don't have any regrets there.

After I got married, I came to Wales and went to university and studied English literature. My journalism lecturer was keen for me to pursue a career in journalism

Family holiday in Dubai, with husband, Ashfaq, celebrating daughter, Zainab's 21st and son, Sulaiman's 19th birthdays, 2020

SEVENTY YEARS OF STRUGGLE AND ACHIEVEMENT  183

The week that I graduated, I found out I was pregnant, so for the next eight months, I decided to work as a journalist for a public relations company in Cardiff, reporting on UK-based companies like BP Oil and their relationship with the global economy. It was an interesting and enjoyable job, and the company wanted me to take on a leadership role. Perhaps it was a missed opportunity with the unfortunate timing of me being pregnant, but it didn't matter, and it didn't bother me. I knew there would be plenty of opportunities later on.

I had my daughter, Zainab, and two years later, my son, Sulaiman, and was a stay-at-home mother for a few years. When my son began school, I started working again. I got a job in the third sector, though at the time, I didn't know much about this kind of work. I was employed at Minority Ethnic Women's Network (MEWN) Cymru, a women's equality organisation, as a project engagement officer, which was like an outreach officer. Within three months, I became a project manager, and six months later, I was managing the

team as the assistant director. A year later, I was asked to go for the director's role because the current director was retiring. I ended up staying there for seven years.

During my time at MEWN, I had a number of different projects, one of which was to deliver a physical activity project for sedentary people. I also adapted my journalistic skills to writing reports and brought in quite a lot of funding. In my final role as director, I also managed the budgets of eight funding bodies.

As part of our partnership working agreement with the Equality and Human Rights Division (EHRD) at the Welsh Assembly Government, I brought together six groups that represented a good cross-section of ethnicity and faith, with a view to educating them on the process of government policy proposals in Wales. I was also asked to be a chair of various other organisations, such as the Wales Women's Network, and I assisted a number of organisations to secure more funding for themselves.

I then moved on to work for a social care organisation called Reach, which was part of the Seren Group (now Pobl). It's very professionally structured and led, with hundreds of staff, and quite different to what I was used to. It was a very busy job, and I did huge amounts of intensive work. As area manager, I was responsible for 120 members of staff within Cardiff, Vale and Rhondda Cynon Taff, and I directly line managed seven team managers. It was a fast-paced environment, and I worked with a lot of talented and professional individuals, but no matter how hard I tried, I just didn't have a passion for the work.

Instead, I moved on to a charity called Race Equality First, and I've been in my current role for the past nine years. The organisation is a 45-year-old charity that supports victims of discrimination, racism and hate crime and delivers projects to promote equality. We help victims to report to the police and to get through the criminal justice system, as well as accessing counselling and any other support that they need.

My job is to ensure that Race Equality First delivers the work it was set up to do, which means that I have to manage the budgets to ensure that we have enough money for our running costs, our staff, and to deliver our work. I coordinate all of the organisation's activities and campaigning and plan how we educate the public about equality. I'm often asked to give advice on equality to other organisations and am invited to speak at public events and conferences. I also do media interviews on TV, radio and for the press when there are racism issues in the news.

I learnt early on in my role, that as a race equality council, we didn't need to be a large organisation, but what is essential is that we do what we do very well if we want to achieve justice for victims of hate and discrimination. So it's my job to make sure everyone in our organisation delivers good services which people want and need, and I review anything that goes out externally to the public or to our funders.

Race equality has made regular headlines over the last year, which has shown us that we've got a long way to go before it can be achieved. Not only do our existing hate crime and equality laws need to be better structured and more effective, but we also need far more targeted action to make equality a reality in so many areas, like health and education. Our research helped to form the Framework for Action on Tackling Hate Crime in 2015, which to this day remains unprecedented, but there is a lot of work to be done to bring the changes we need, and the slow progress is very frustrating.

I've had many challenges in my current role, and have had to face a lot of difficult situations, sometimes even standing up to bullies. But I'm happy for these challenges because I'm a much stronger woman as a result. I've also learnt not to waste time worrying about things I can't change and to either move on or try to repair the situation.

Aliya at work at Race Equality First, 2019

Aliya recording an interview with ITV about a racial hate crime

It's good to plan ahead, but you should know that things don't always go to plan, and if they don't, things always work out in the end, often better than what was initially planned.

For me, the key has always been to do only what I enjoy doing for a living. I know I've been lucky to find this, but it's the best advice I can give. If you enjoy your job, it will motivate you, make you learn faster, and you'll naturally want to do it well, which will help you to succeed in any role.

# Youthful Engagement

## Alka Ahuja
**CONSULTANT CHILD AND ADOLESCENT PSYCHIATRIST**

*If I've set my heart on something, I will do it. Each time I fail, I work much harder. I don't let go, and each time I'm pushed, I come back ten times stronger.*

Alka with her parents; sister, Kamni and brother, Rajiv, 1985

I was born in Bombay, India and was the youngest of three siblings. I went to a convent school and always listened and was well behaved. I went on to be the head girl of the school and was quite ambitious and did well academically, despite being a worrier.

I had always wanted to do medicine, although I came from a totally non-medical background. My father was a businessman and my mother was a teacher, but she gave up her job to bring up the three of us. Medicine was not something that was recommended by anybody in the family, but I was determined. Medicine was quite competitive, and to get in, you had to be among the cream of the cream. Most of my peers went for extra classes and tuition, but I was actually discouraged by my family from doing this because of my anxious temperament. I did it all on my own, as I was determined. I did very well and ended up getting the gold medal in biology.

I absolutely loved medicine, though it was very hard, and in the first six months, for the first time ever, I failed one of my exams, which felt like the end of the world. But I'm a tough cookie, and I retook it and passed. I knew I didn't want to just do medicine; I wanted to excel at it. Unfortunately, in my last year of medicine, while I was preparing for my final exams, my father died suddenly, and it was hard because I was particularly close to him. As a family, we were coming to terms with it, and my mum was finding it really hard. But she stood by me and I did well in the exams, but not as well as I could have done.

I'd always wanted to do something with children and loved talking and listening to people who would confide in me. So, when I did psychiatry during my internship, I immediately fell in love with it, as I thought it's a speciality that can make a huge difference to people's lives. I did my psychiatry training in Bombay, and during my MD, I worked with street children in the city, which was something that was close to my heart and I was very passionate about. A lot of these children not only have psychological issues but basic physical issues, like lack of food and exposure to infection. I tried to put in a support network with the health services that were around, which was difficult because the moment somebody tried to help them, these kids would move on to another city. I recently got involved in some work regarding poverty and street children in this country, although things are slightly different compared to India.

In the end, when I graduated, I received a first and was the gold medallist in psychiatry at Bombay University. It was hard, but my mother stood by me at every stage and helped me prove that I could do it and made me believe in myself. I went on to get my first psychiatry job, which was a bit of teaching, as well as clinical work and research.

At this point, I was 28, and a lot of my friends were

Working with Bombay street children

beginning to settle down and have children. One thing I was sure of was that I would have an arranged marriage. People have very different views about arranged marriages, but it's not something that you're forced into. It's decided mutually by the two families and the relationship extends beyond the two people to include their wider families too.

My mum arranged for me to meet somebody who was in Wales doing medical specialist training. We met when he returned for a family visit, and we clicked. We got engaged within five days and married within six months in Bombay. We're very different characters. We often joke that we have very little in common, as he loves his sports and music, which I don't, but that is the secret of our happy marriage. We've been married for 22 years and have two children.

When we got married, I'd never had a career break, so I thought I would take six months off to set up the house in Swansea and get used to the place. I came to Wales in September and it was miserable weather— rainy and cold, but I got used to it. I had friends in this country, but all of them were working. I used to call them up and have a chat on weekends or evenings, but within a month, I realised this was not for me and that I needed to get back to work.

I was lucky because when I met with the consultant who would be responsible for my psychiatry training, he was quite impressed with my CV, and I managed to get on a psychiatry rotation quickly and promptly passed the exams.

Wedding day, Bombay, 1998

I started my child psychiatry training and then got pregnant with my first child. It was difficult because my husband was in Nottingham doing a fellowship, so I was on my own and was not very well during the pregnancy. But I had fantastic neighbours at that time, including a retired nurse who would come round every evening to ensure I'd eaten and would bring me cakes and sandwiches.

Then my father-in-law had a heart attack, and my husband had to rush back to India and was away for some time. We were moving house, and I was trying to get the new house ready for the baby, and trying to do things on my own. My daughter is lovely and I love her, but it was hard work, as she didn't sleep or feed well. But during this time, I finished my training, got a consultant job and then my son was born.

I absolutely adore them both and wouldn't have swapped the

situation for anything, but it was challenging. Over the years, I had a lot of opportunities and could have done much more in my career, but I had no support in place for childcare. My children are in their teens now, and probably once they're grown up and in university, I will get opportunities to do more.

At the moment, I do three days' clinical work at the Aneurin Bevan University Health Board and run a tertiary neuro-developmental service for children with autism and ADHD, doing assessments and looking at what support can be made available. We've developed apps and a digital sound walk, which will help in different environments to support them. We're currently working on a virtual reality tool. I also do a lot of work with the Welsh Government on advising policies and services for children and young people with autism and ADHD. I work late hours and weekends, but I don't mind. If I've set my heart on something, I will do it.

I was also the chair for Child Psychiatry at the Royal College of Psychiatrists in Wales, and I'm now the Public Education lead, so I do a lot of work with schools and the public, and we run a lot of debates for young people on mental health topics. We work very closely with third-sector education and local authorities, trying to support mental health and wellbeing among young people. Things are changing and improving, but there's a long way to go.

I've had many opportunities, and people have been very supportive, but I think being a woman and from an ethnic minority, you almost have to work twice as hard. Unfortunately, the media doesn't help because when

Alka with the Royal College of Psychiatrists, Wales Career Fair, February 2020

people think about countries like India, they think about snake charmers and poverty and street children and people being uneducated. But I went to an excellent school, and I speak six languages, but there have been times when people have just looked and thought, can you do it? And I think the only way you can prove it is

Alka with husband, Sashin; son, Ansh and daughter, Saiba, on a family holiday at Disney Florida, 2017

SEVENTY YEARS OF STRUGGLE AND ACHIEVEMENT   191

by doing it. I've got lovely friends here, and we socialise and have a good network, but sometimes I've felt like I don't fit in here, and when I've gone back to India, things have moved on there as well, and I don't fit in. But in other ways, I've got the best of both worlds.

I'm a very strong believer in God, and I get a lot of strength from that. I've faced disappointments and failures and have missed opportunities, but I don't give up. It's important to believe in yourself and not to give up. It's a hard, bumpy ride, but if you have set your mind on something, just go for it. It might take long, but it is achievable, and if you've got a dream, pursue it.

I have a motivational quote up on my office wall: 'Mirror, mirror on the wall. I will get up each time I fall. Whether I walk, run or crawl. I'll set my aims and achieve them all.' I just think each time I fail, I work much harder. I'm almost like a dog with a bone. I just don't let go, and each time I'm pushed, I come back ten times stronger.

# In the Spirit of Learning

## Norma Glass
**JEWISH COMMUNITY LEADER AND DIVERSITY TRAINING EDUCATOR**

*If you want to have a positive future, you need to look back to see where your character comes from. It's also important to have an education, which is something you can carry with you wherever you are in life and that nobody can take away from you.*

I was born in Swansea to Jewish parents. My childhood was rather different. My parents had a grocery store, and we lived in a flat over the shop. I lived in a very poor area, and most of my friends, if they had shoes, they were somebody else's, so my friends thought that I was very wealthy because my parents had a shop. They didn't realise that my father went to bed after midnight and got up every day at 4 o'clock in the morning, and we never had a holiday or a day off because business was 24/7.

I had a wonderful childhood, but because I was Jewish and was fat, I had problems. It wasn't so much that I was the only Jewish child in the village, but that I was a fat, Jewish child. I became the court jester, and I would make jokes about myself before anybody else did. It hurt to be called things like, 'You fat Jew', but it was the fat part that worried me more, as I always wanted to be like my friends.

I loved infants' school because, despite the fact I was Jewish, I was always chosen to be Mary, the mother of Jesus in the nativity play, because I was a big girl and taller than the others, at least until I went on to the next school. The only time a lot of those children ever had any extra treat to look forward to was Christmas. They used to say to me, 'What are you having for Christmas?' Because I was Jewish, we didn't have Christmas, but my birthday was in December, so I would tell them whatever I was given for my birthday, so I got that feeling of equality.

I went to grammar school and was considered to be quite bright. I liked arts subjects, like languages, history,

Norma, age 5

geography—any subject I could write essays and sort of answer in a roundabout way. There was a drive at schools at that time to make any bright person go into science because they were looking for scientists. I had a Jewish boyfriend then who wanted to be a doctor, so I thought it would be lovely if I became a doctor too. So I did science, but I really struggled with physics, and in the end, I decided to do pharmacy.

I think those of my era thought in terms of getting married and having children because that was what was expected of them, especially in Jewish families. When I went into upper sixth, I met another boy who was to become my future husband. He was older than me and a qualified architect, and he must have been very bright because he went into university at the age of sixteen, which wouldn't happen today. We got married in 1963 when I was 24 and had a big wedding.

I then did a speech and drama degree at the London Royal Academy of Music and Dramatic Art, and I got my teaching diploma. When I was pregnant with my first daughter, Deborah, I was teaching speech at a school in Swansea, and though I was wearing a loose coat, when I stretched to write something on the board, a young man at the back pointed out to the whole class that I was having a baby. It was very weird, but in those days, you hid pregnancy rather than promoting it. So I thought I'd best forget class teaching and do some teaching at home instead. So while I was teaching children speech at home, I put my daughter Deborah in a highchair, which was all right until her box of Smarties had been eaten, so that was the end of that. I stayed at home, and in time, had a second daughter, Judith.

Norma's wedding day, 1963

I still had a love of the arts, so I decided to study interior design and was employed by other architects, though never by my husband, I have to say. I really enjoyed that, and I was in my element. However, I was very much a stay-at-home mum, so I could only do local work. Swansea was not a place of affluence in those days. There weren't that many people who had grand homes who wanted interior designers. So, I did restaurant work, but there weren't that many restaurants then in the 1960s. The days of the Chinese and Indian restaurants hadn't come in yet.

When I was almost 40, I thought I would do something part-time related to skincare, so I worked for Charles of the Ritz, one of the most popular make-up houses at the time. Then I worked for Yves St Laurent, promoting Opium perfume, which I still wear. I had a wonderful time promoting Yves St Laurent fragrance and skincare. I would say to customers, 'Now, Madam, it's all very well spending this money on an outfit, but what about your face?' I was good at sales, and they would buy these pots of cream with magic ingredients.

I actually retired from outside work at the age of 50. I began giving talks at the synagogue to rotary clubs, church groups and many visiting groups of school pupils. I used to wear a hat because Jewish women cover their heads in the synagogue, and a number of times, particularly the little ones, would say, 'Miss, are you the Queen?' And I used to say, 'No, the Queen is much older than me.' We have the Torah, a huge Biblical scroll made of goatskin on two wooden poles. There was a particular Torah that was over 300 years old, but because it was damaged, I could show it to the kids and let them touch the old goatskin and explain to them how we read Hebrew backwards.

I did these talks in the synagogue for 30 years, up until about ten years ago. Our community got too small to maintain the building's upkeep, so the synagogue was sold to the LifePoint Church, though we still use the building for worship. The LifePoint Church do brilliant Christian work among the community, and we have a truly wonderful relationship with them—the best example of Jews and Christians working together and respecting each other. They are so kind to us, and we appreciate everything they do.

For twenty years, I was also on the board of deputies of British Jews, a governing body representing British Jewry. I used to have to go to London once a month for meetings. I stopped when I was 70, only because I used to hear people standing at the mic saying, 'In my day, we did it this way,' and I thought, get out before you say it. Now I visit schools quite a lot and do a virtual tour of the synagogue and talk about being a Jew. It's about educating to dispel ignorance. If people hear that certain faiths do things that they think are weird, they get frightened and begin to dislike, and dislike turns to hatred, and that's how you get problems. That's why I do diversity training, working with interfaith organisations and universities wherever I can.

Norma receiving an MBE from the Queen for her work on racial diversity, 2003

There have been anti-Semitic incidents, though, without a doubt. One time I went into the synagogue, and the whole place had been vandalised with obscene writing and swastikas everywhere. It wasn't very nice, but I believe you douse flames—you don't add oxygen. I thought we should just get going the next week and be back in business with services, which we were, so they had lost the battle in that way.

Norma with the Lord Mayor of Swansea, 2018

Jewish people came to Swansea from 1700 onwards. The city was a sanctuary for my grandparents when they came, and we're still going now. My grandfather and his brother had been taken by force into the Russian Army at the age of nine. They both escaped and swam across a river. His brother drowned, but my grandfather survived, and God knows how he got from there to Cardiff docks. This has made me grounded and realise that I wouldn't be here, that there was a sacrifice made which, for me, goes back further than the Holocaust. Most of my family were wiped out in Germany, but my grandparents made it here.

My family is also unique in that my grandmother was the only female Jewish farmer in the whole country. She was up at 5 o'clock every morning and went with the men to milk a herd of cows. She never stopped working all day and my parents were the same, so I had the work ethic, but I didn't have to do it the way that they did. I mean, I feel guilty now, even at the age of 80, that I'm not working, though I'm doing voluntary things.

I was very fortunate in life that I had wonderful parents and grandparents. But the most important thing was that I was fortunate enough to have a husband who was fantastic, and he was somebody who let me fly, and I think because he let me do things, my prime instinct was to come back home.

You don't come here as an island. You've got a background and people around you in the present. And if you want to have a positive future, you need to look back to see where your character comes from and change it, improve it, or wish for a better life, which is what most good parents want for their children.

Jewish families started off with nothing and came here with nothing. They did the best they could and always tried to give their children an education. That's why I feel that whatever you do with your life, you've got to have an education. It doesn't have to be university. It can be any craft, as long as you've got something you can carry with you wherever you are in life—nobody can take it away from you.

Norma featured with First Minister of Wales, Carwyn Jones, upon receipt of a Lifetime Achievement Award for her work in race relations, 2010

**196** SEVENTY YEARS OF STRUGGLE AND ACHIEVEMENT

# A World of Healthy Diversity

## Diana De
**SENIOR LECTURER, ADULT NURSING**

*People sometimes find it difficult to talk about culture for fear of offending, but I think it is important to encourage conversations around difference and diversity. Culture isn't just about ethnicity or being a different skin colour. It's more interesting, fluid and highly complex and about what we're born into and what moulds us into the individuals who we later become.*

I was born in Edinburgh in 1974. I'm the eldest child and was named after the singer Diana Ross, and my younger sister after Debbie Harry, from Blondie. My parents are of Indian heritage, but broke tradition and had a love marriage rather than an arranged one. They came to the UK in the 1960s, and I spent most of my childhood in Carlisle, Cumbria, near the Lake District.

My parents were quite liberal with us growing up, but there was one tradition that they followed which had a real impact on me. Boys and girls of Indian descent normally get their head shaved at a young age to remove their invitro baby hair. As a child, I had lovely, thick, curly hair, and my parents were reluctant to do this to me. They eventually caved in after my grandparents visited from India and persuaded them. So, at the age of five, my head was shaved, and for much of that year, I looked like a mini Sinead O'Connor. We'd also moved to a new house around that time, and I remember being mistaken by the local kids as the 'new boy from number 20'.

Typically, in Asian culture, boys are favoured over girls, but my sister and I had a lot of freedom and fun, and I enjoyed my childhood. We lived on a quiet cul-de-sac in a corner house with a large garden, a Sheltie dog, and a welcoming open-house approach. We always had visitors, and all the kids used to come over to our place to play. I would be out all day with my friends, climbing trees, throwing balls, walking on stilts and skateboarding. I love natural history, and we lived near a local wood, so I'd go off to the countryside and ride my bike for miles. I also read a great deal, and my sister and I were privileged to have gone on plenty of overseas family holidays.

I have fond childhood memories of aromatic cooking smells drifting through our house, but back then, my sister and I used to complain and demanded English food, such

Diana, age 9

as fish fingers, like all our friends used to eat. Nowadays, I greatly miss Mum's Indian dishes and have grown up to appreciate just how good a cook she is.

My father was an orthopaedic specialist from a long line of doctors, his father having been nominated for a Nobel Prize for advancements in medicine and the treatment of cholera. My dad worked very long hours, and much of his evenings were spent on call, but he found time to do things like take me to watch the hospital fireworks and give out presents to the patients on Christmas Day. My mother was a nurse who predominantly worked night shifts to accommodate my father's rota. They worked hard and have both been strong positive role models.

Growing up, I was the only brown-skinned girl in my school, so I stood out and was sometimes self-conscious about being different. I recall being anxious around certain boys who would call me names, and harassment was practically a part of my everyday life. However, as I grew up, being different became a positive thing and more exotic, with people becoming more interested in my family origins. As an adult, I've never felt that being female or labelled BAME has ever stopped me from achieving anything professionally or personally. My mum also maintained that race or colour would not be factors in either of her girls' success. If we worked hard, it would pay off, and we would succeed based on our merit. If, however, we didn't achieve, we'd simply have to try again. I personally view Britain and British people to be relatively tolerant. I've occasionally heard others play the race card, which makes me feel uncomfortable and often leads me to challenge such suggestions.

When I left school, I didn't really know what I wanted to be. I went through phases where I wanted to be a newsreader or an air hostess. Eventually, my parents suggested nursing and getting a job helping at the local infirmary, and I found that I liked it. In 1993, I went to study nursing at Northumbria University in Newcastle. Although there weren't many people like me in my student nurse cohort, the bigger northern city was much more multicultural than I'd been used to. Once I completed my training, I worked in general medicine and cardiology before I went on to obtain my degree. I then decided to change to intensive care nursing, which became my speciality. I revelled in this highly charged environment and felt supported by the camaraderie I shared with my team.

After eight fun-filled years in Newcastle, in 2000, I decided to go to Australia for a year. I obtained a Young Person's working visa and took a chance to go there without a job lined up. Luckily, I managed to find nursing jobs, including one in a critical care unit in New South Wales. I attended the Sydney Olympics, and the same year, on my birthday, I met and fell in love with an Aussie called Jon, a computer scientist living in Melbourne. When my visa expired the following year, I returned to Newcastle somewhat heartbroken. Nevertheless, our long-distance relationship continued.

Jon eventually joined me in the UK in 2002 and took up a job at Cardiff University, while I found work locally at the University Hospital Wales in their critical care unit. Part of my role was to mentor student nurses, while I also took on some lunchtime teaching sessions for fellow staff members. At the time, some of my clinical colleagues and course tutors suggested I consider a lecturing role, and, as luck would have it, an academic job came up at the University of Glamorgan (now the University of South Wales) to teach Nurse Education. Although it was only a one-year contract, they decided to keep me on afterwards. Jon and I moved from Cardiff to the Welsh Valleys, so I'd have less of a commute, and it was only there that, as a mixed-race couple, we struggled to settle or feel we belonged. Our form of escapism was to travel extensively, which included the pleasure of seeing many rare animals in the wild.

We got married in 2005, and our wedding took place in a beautiful setting in the Lake District. I was struck by the diversity of our guests, as people had travelled from far and wide to be there with us. Our honeymoon was a round-the-world trip, which included another wedding celebration in Jon's mother's beautiful rainforest back garden in Australia.

Just before we got married, I had obtained a prestigious travel scholarship from the Florence Nightingale Foundation to research sickle cell disorders in Jamaica and Cuba and continued this work in America the following year, courtesy of the Welsh Intensive Care Society. I remember presenting my scholarship findings in London, and I think I was the only 'melanin enriched' girl that got up on stage. I wanted this to change, so I became proactive in encouraging more nurses like me from BAME backgrounds to apply for these opportunities. I worked with the Foundation and Chief Nursing Officer for Wales to bolster more interest. In 2006, I was subsequently honoured to be asked to 'carry the lamp' at the annual Florence Nightingale commemoration service. Being in the spotlight in front of 2,000 people at Westminster Abbey was daunting but one of my proudest achievements. The occasion was made even more special, as my parents were there, my mum having just retired from the NHS after 40 years, so I felt as though I was continuing the nursing journey for her.

Diana on a trip to Africa, 2004

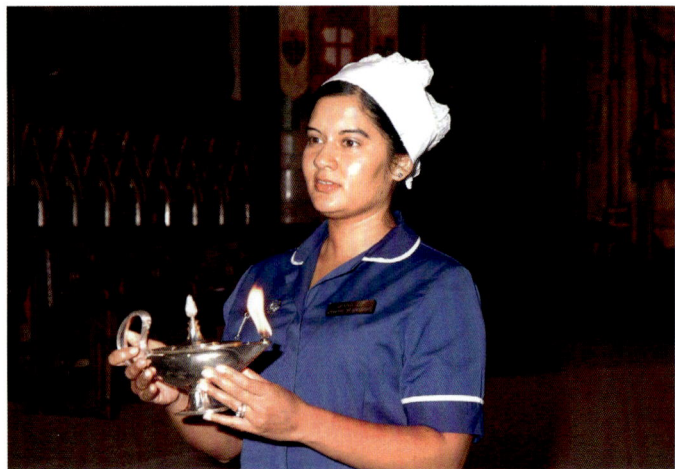

Diana at the Florence Nightingale Commemoration Service, 2006

Around this time, I gave birth to my first child. We moved back to Cardiff, and eighteen months later, our son came along. He was born with a hole in the heart and required open-heart surgery before he was one year old. This was an extremely challenging time for us as a family, but he recovered brilliantly. All my children are doing well. My eldest daughter is a flautist, like my sister, and dances classical Indian dancing with grace. My son is now eleven and is a healthy, active, quick-witted boy who's into football, gaming and music. Just after my 40th birthday, we had our third child. She is delightful and sassy and has been a wonderful addition to our family.

In 2008, I decided to undertake a Master's degree. I studied equality and diversity and tailored my dissertation to the topic of improving pedagogy around internationalisation. I was pleased to attain a Distinction. I also completed my post-grad teaching certificate and, in 2016, secured a permanent teaching position at the School of Healthcare Sciences at Cardiff University. I enjoy teaching, as it allows me to increase awareness of important health issues related to cultural safety by raising the profile of haemoglobinopathy disorders and safeguarding vulnerable people linked to traditional harmful practices, like female genital mutilation, honour-based violence and modern-day slavery. These topics can sometimes be ethnocentrically perceived, but my campaign is for these to be seen from more of a public health and protection viewpoint.

Through my teaching, I came to be involved with the EMWWAA mentorship programme, and in 2019, I was an EMWWAA finalist for contributions made to STEM learning. The nomination was linked to my efforts in promoting healthcare education within local primary schools. Every year, I love going to speak to school children and feeding off their enthusiasm to learn. I've since extended my endeavours to local community and secondary school pupils through the Grangetown and Cathays High School Project, which aims to give sixth-formers an insight into healthcare careers and is an opportunity to present myself as a relatable role model. As a woman of colour, I'd like to influence more people like me to consider nursing or healthcare as worthy career options, and I will continue to work tirelessly to reduce race-related stigma and barriers.

Change is occurring, and nowadays, I see more male students in my classes, as well as those from BAME backgrounds. I'm currently working with colleagues to develop a podcast that aims to help encourage more people from under-represented groups into the profession or to progress further in their careers.

On reflection, nursing was the right choice for me, and I still enjoy what I do. I've helped many graduate students become fully-fledged nurses and supported international nurses to register in the UK and those who've had a break from nursing to return back to clinical practice.

For me, culture and diversity are worth celebrating, and I think it's so important for youngsters today to learn about

Diana with husband, Jon, at the EMMWHA Awards, 2019

their heritage. Many different cultural aspects have shaped me into a global citizen, like travel, music, food and literature, as well as my work and my family. I enjoy walking and painting in my free time, as well as cooking and sharing food with friends. Although I regret not sticking with viola lessons or teaching my kids to be fluent in Bengali, I can reflect upon most of my life experiences with positivity. It's fantastic to hear that my Vegemite-infused children tell me I'm a role model to them. To me, they are far more self-assured than I was at their age and don't recognise differences in culture, language or skin colour as adversities. I hope, as parents, we've supported their sense of self-worth and respect for others, along with the importance of family and trying to remain healthy and happy in all the choices they make in their lives.

My advice is to focus, but remain open to new ideas, work hard, and believe that anything can be possible. Life is all about celebrating and maintaining a balance, and enjoying whatever you do. I hope my story helps to influence and encourage others in some meaningful way.

# Portuguese Flavours

## Iolanda Banu Viegas
**COUNCILLOR OF THE UK PORTUGUESE COMMUNITY**

*Always follow your dreams and do what your conscience tells you to do. Even when we hit the ground, when we find our strength to come back to the top that's what makes us stronger.*

I was born in Mozambique in 1974. When I was six, I moved with my mother to Portugal and started school when I was seven. At the time, I didn't speak much Portuguese, but within a few weeks, I began to read and write fluently and became one of the best Portuguese students in the school. I also used to be very good at sports—gymnastics and running.

When I was around ten or eleven, I was hit by a car, and I was in a coma for a year. I had to learn to walk and do everything again. Because I'd missed a whole year of school, I lost a bit of the motivation I'd previously had. But maybe because I was young, I had that will to live, and a year later, I won a marathon in my age group, so that gave me a different sort of boost. I think the accident was something that changed my life forever because I learned at a very young age that something bad can happen within seconds and we're not going to be here forever, so it's better we do something good while we're here, rather than leave it for later.

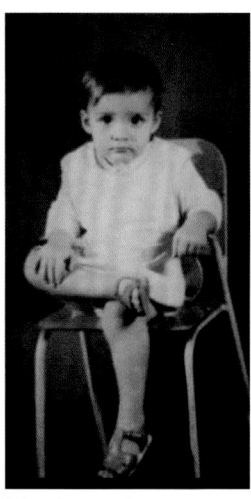

Iolanda, age 3, Mozambique, 1977

When I left school, I had jobs working behind a bar serving customers. I was always very good with people, and even if they were in a bad mood, I could cheer them up. At age 26, I was already running my own bar. It was successful, but I was working all hours of the day and never had a day off and was very tired. I saw a job advertised in the UK working in a London warehouse. It sounded very easy and well paid. I decided that since all my favourite bands came from the UK, I'd go for six months.

The next day I caught a flight and came to the UK on my own. This was January 2001.

From the airport, an agency bus took about 50 of us Portuguese, dropping us off in different places. I was sure I was going to be working in London, but we drove for about five or six hours and got to Wrexham in the middle of the night. I had no idea where I was, but at least I had made a friend on the bus who stayed with me.

The next day I went to open a bank account, and I was reading signs, thinking, nobody ever told us that they speak a different language in Wales. What is Wales in the first place, because all they taught us about was England. And the job wasn't in a warehouse—it was a meatpacking factory with freezing cold temperatures. I'd only brought summery clothes from Portugal and didn't have any boots or a parka—things I'd need both for work and the snowy weather outside.

We worked in lines, packing meat onto nice plates. It was very repetitive, but the salary was good. One of my colleagues on the line was a big man in his 60s from Nigeria. He'd had a heart attack but came back to work because he was worried if he didn't, he would be replaced by someone else. I felt so sorry for him that I was doing all of his work as well as mine, and I damaged my back and couldn't work. Somebody took me to a GP, and the doctor gave me a sick note to hand over the following day. The manager told me I couldn't present a sick note or have sick pay because I'd been working there for less than six months. I didn't know what to do. I wasn't ready to go home. There was so much to explore. I hadn't even had the chance to go to a proper concert like I'd wanted.

Someone took me to the council with the letter from my doctor, and a couple of weeks later, the council got me my first flat and all the furniture. I'd never been so happy in my life. It would be perfect if the entire world had this system because this doesn't happen in Portugal. I got a job at a pizza factory, which paid three times what I was earning before. Then, all the Portuguese people were asking, how did I do it? I met people who needed to go to the doctor, pregnant women who didn't know what to do, domestic violence victims. So I started volunteering as a Portuguese interpreter for Bawso (Black Association of Women Step Out).

In 2010, I formed Comunidade de Lingua Portuguesa de Wrexham (CLPW), a Portuguese-language speakers' group. A few years ago, we became a community interest company, which makes it easier for us to access funding to do the activities we want to do. We work with elderly people who are quite isolated and don't know what's going on around the neighbourhood. They're still watching Portuguese television, and they only know news about their home countries. We also work with people in Wrexham of all ages and from eight different Portuguese-speaking countries—Portugal, Mozambique, Angola, Cape Verde, Guinea, Timor, São Tomé and Príncipe and Brazil.

There are not many of us—a few hundred—but we're all facing the same problems, like language and not knowing the laws and obligations, so we try to break those barriers, and try to teach the adults English and basic computer

Iolanda at the launch of *Our Story,* a CLPW booklet published in Portuguese, English and Welsh about the Portuguese diaspora of Wrexham, 2019

Iolanda at St David's Day celebrations with students from Welsh-language classes provided by CLPW, in partnership with College Cambria, 2020

skills. But we also try to integrate, so we bring our Welsh neighbours to do activities with our Portuguese. We understand that if we know each other, it's much easier for us to get on better. If I know my neighbours, I tend not to feel afraid of them anymore, so I thought if people got to know a bit more of the Portuguese culture, a bit of our food and drink, maybe they would accept us better.

When you're born into such a diverse family, you don't feel there are differences. Outsiders start to tell you things that you were never aware of in your life. I found out in this country that I'm mixed race. I grew up thinking I was maybe white in Mozambique and whatever I wanted to be in Portugal.

Wales is my home now, like Portugal was before, like Mozambique was before that. I don't actually own a country, and it's not mine. My home is where I am, where I feel happy. But I might want to go back to Mozambique to resume my humanitarian missions and carry on doing what I've always done —helping people.

I was also elected a councillor representative for Portuguese people living in the UK. I'm one of the four women out of the 86 Portuguese councillors all over the world. I'm very good at community activism, and being the first one actually doing something because if it doesn't exist, someone has to do it; so instead of waiting for someone to do it, I decide to do it myself.

I never thought, in a million years, I would get the awards that I did. Most of it took me by surprise. I do it for different kinds of rewards; the reward that makes me feel happy makes me sleep in peace. Every time I do something for someone, I've helped myself as well because I learn so much about everything.

Iolanda receiving an EMWWAA award in the Self-Development category, 2019

Iolanda as Chair of Black History Month, North Wales, at an event in Wrexham, 2016

Nothing I do is for money. Personal gain for me is how we reach other people's lives. I know people I meet through my life—it won't be easy for them to forget me, but not because I give them £1 million. It's because maybe I see life in a different way, the most basic, simple way.

Every day is a challenge. We learn how to be strong when we feel these difficulties in our skins. For instance, hate crimes I've felt in my skin so many times, so I've put a shield around me. But I see that this is not my problem. If someone has a problem with me, they're the ones who need education and support. I'm glad at least my daughter, she's very good with her studies, and I really want her to follow a different route because my life is not that easy—it's full of struggles.

Nothing lasts forever, so whatever happens with us, it is part of our journey, and that's what makes our experiences of life, and what makes us strong and what makes us weak. We are what we want to be, and I've learned from all of these experiences. I take everything—good or bad, and I learn how to deal with things, as we need to make the most of opportunities.

My advice is to always follow your dreams and do what your conscience tells you to do. Don't listen to what other people say. They might give you good and bad advice, so take your own decisions and never say that you can't do it.

One thing I know is, if you just do things right you will never know how it is to fail or how it feels to be down. Even if you fail, if you follow your conscience you're always right. Because it's usually when we fail, when we hit the ground, that we find our strength to come back to the top, and that's what makes us stronger.

# Strength in Diversity

## Abi Lasebikan
**DIVERSITY AND INCLUSION OFFICER**

*I get a lot of satisfaction from improving things so people can be themselves and work in an environment where they are welcome and feel included, regardless of who they are and what they do. It's our differences that make us unique, and that uniqueness is to be cherished and celebrated.*

I was born in Ikeja, Lagos, West Africa, and have an older sister and younger brother. My childhood was full of colour, music, food and events involving music and dancing. My mum is from Wales, and we used to come here quite regularly to visit my nan, so I had that dual culture. I can honestly say that I've been blessed to have experienced life on two continents and having all the marvellous experiences that the two cultures have provided me with.

At the age of nine, I came permanently to the UK to a specialist boarding school in Kent for people with dyslexia. It wasn't easy for me. I was quite studious and had always been a bookworm, but reading wasn't something that came naturally to me and took me longer. I had extra tuition and had to work and study hard. My dad wanted us all to get a British education because it was considered an advantage to have one. In Nigeria, there would be a lot of teacher strikes that would go on for months, so your education would be interrupted, but also, recognition-wise, at that time, British education had a bit higher kudos.

My siblings and I all went to boarding school. I was the last to go into boarding school and the first to leave because I was homesick. I'd read *Mallory Towers*, with the midnight picnics and pranks on the tutors and matrons, so I had this idea of what boarding school was going to be like, but it wasn't—the reality was something else. My mum had also come back to the UK permanently, so it made no sense for us to be in boarding school anymore.

Abi, around age 6, on a visit to her grandmother in Wales

Abi, around age 16, on a visit to the family home in Nigeria

I went to high school in Penarth, and after I graduated, I decided to go to university but didn't want to go somewhere local. I chose Edge Hill University, in a little town called Ormskirk, between Liverpool and Manchester, which was one of those unique places that seemed to have a pub or hairdresser on every corner. It was a lovely place with lovely people. I studied applied social science and community relations, also studying criminology and mental health in my final year.

When I finished university, I came back to Cardiff, the idea being to travel and to take a year's break. However, I ended up getting a job and got used to the income. I never did the year's break and have been in work ever since. For a while, I did direct sales and marketing. I would knock on people's doors, selling discount cards, which I think made me very good at interacting with a range of people. In cold calling, you've only got a few minutes to win people over and explain why it's a good idea that they should hand you money, so I credit that period with acquiring the ability to comfortably interact with different people.

Now I'm a diversity and inclusion officer. I'd like to say that becoming a diversity officer was my plan all along, but it happened quite inadvertently. I was searching for a career that I enjoyed and that enriched me. After doing direct sales, I worked in a call centre for a major gas company but discovered it was not for me. That's how I went to work in the civil service, working in a few different departments.

During my time in the civil service, I took a career break to study law and qualified as a solicitor, which I did in spite of my dyslexia, and I'm very proud of this achievement. Working as a legal assistant did not satisfy me, so when a post on the diversity and inclusion (D&I) team came up where I'd been working, I grabbed the opportunity and never looked back. I was able to put to use all the skills I had gained up to this point and make a difference, so you could say that it was fate, and the role found me.

Our department provides strategic direction, and I support people in the organisation, deliver training, and raise awareness on diversity and inclusion issues. We work to achieve accreditations, which highlight the organisation's commitment to diversity and inclusion. We work closely with the other departments to embed

Abi being admitted onto the roll of solicitors in England and Wales, 2012

Abi giving a presentation as part of a 'Careers and Employability Disability Employer' panel organised by Cardiff University and GO Wales, 2019

diversity and inclusion and to create a culture of belonging. Our main focus is ensuring that we meet our public duty under the Equality Act 2010 and inclusivity, and we're conscious of things like socio-economic inequality and intersectionality.

In addition to my full-time D&I officer role, I was the chair of Race, Ethnicity and Cultural Heritage (REACH) for over four years. REACH is a members' led workplace equality network providing peer support, networking opportunities and a space to discuss issues affecting Black, Asian and minority ethnic members in the organisation. I also liaise closely with other workplace equality networks and have worked with various organisations, like Stonewall and the National Autistic Society.

Right now, diversity and inclusion are on people's minds, and organisations are focused on them, but who knows where this will be in ten years' time. Will there still be diversity and inclusion officers or teams? I suppose that in an ideal world, we would get to a place where there is no need for a specific diversity and inclusion team. However, we still have a long way to go, so I don't think that I'll be out of a job anytime soon.

Winning the EMWWAA award was a pleasant surprise. So often, this kind of work goes unrecognised and unrewarded, and people don't realise the hard work that a lot of people put in and the good that they do. It was a great honour and one of my crowning moments.

For me, there's a certain level of job satisfaction that comes with giving back. I've been quite fortunate with the support that my parents

A proud and ecstatic Abi with her EMMWAA award in the Self-Development category, 2019

gave me, but also, my experiences have made me very aware that it's not necessarily an equal world. So, I get a lot of satisfaction from enabling steps to be made to improve things so that people can be themselves, working in an environment where they are welcome and feel included, regardless of who they are and what they do.

I think if I could have realised what I wanted to do a bit earlier, it would have made the process a lot quicker, without so many distractions or deviations. But I think it has given me a broader range of experience and knowledge to draw on, which is a good thing, so I don't think the deviations were a mistake at all. They've made me who I am and also got me where I am today, so nothing was a waste of time. It's all valuable experience and knowledge.

I would say to people starting out to not be afraid to try different things because you truly won't know where your heart or passion lies until you can try things out. Get as many different experiences as you can under your belt, understand what you want and where your strengths lie because we all have strengths. Then do something that utilises that strength, and your confidence will build. It's very helpful to get someone who's like a mentor or sponsor that will help you through your journey and take you under their wing, even if it's just to seek advice and talk things through. Having someone like that is really valuable. Remember, it's our differences that make us unique, and uniqueness is to be cherished and celebrated. It would be a boring place if we were all the same, so embrace that uniqueness about you.

# Developing care

## Versha Sood
**DEMENTIA SME AND OPERATIONAL LEAD**

*A person who's got passion is already empowered enough to take their passion forward. It's important to have a person that you look up to and to follow their advice, but have your own ways of making a difference and evolve from where you were yesterday and just keep evolving.*

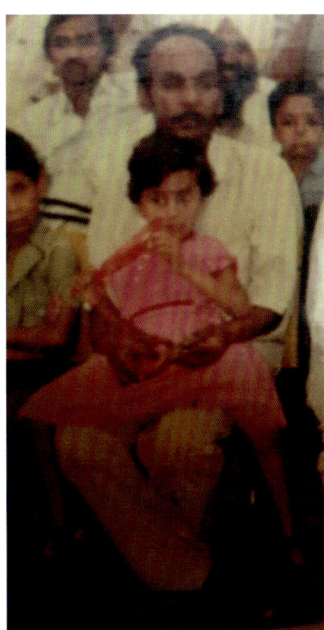

Versha, age 5 with her father in Ludhiana, Punjab, 1984

I was born in the Punjab, India, and have a brother and a sister. My father was in the army, and my mother was a housewife. I had a very ordinary childhood. I loved school and was very academic and very active in sports as well. I had an equal interest in learning household chores, embroidery, crochet, stitching, painting, and so on, and I helped my mother at home and learnt from her how to manage my time from my very early childhood. Family continues to be very important to me. Being married to a progressive-thinking and understanding husband while also having supportive in-laws have made my journey a lot easier and happier too.

I had always wanted to do something in the healthcare sector, and my parents encouraged me to do a nursing qualification, a shorter journey than medicine which could have taken me up to nine years to establish myself. I got a scholarship to do nursing and was also able to study my dream subjects of sociology and history, followed by a Master's in English literature. During this period, my father passed away, and I became the major breadwinner of the family. I took up a full-time job in Chandigarh Government College and taught IELTS part-time, an English language test for people interested in coming abroad.

At one time, I accompanied some of my students to interviews in the UK and decided I wanted to stay here. So I

Versha and her husband, Aditya Mahindra, on their wedding day, 2013

came to Wales in 2005 with a five-year work permit that led to me becoming a permanent citizen. I was initially sponsored by a healthcare company to be a frontline worker supporting people with dementia in care homes. After a few months, I became a team leader, and within three years, became a manager of a care home and a peripatetic manager covering 25 care homes nationwide. My development continued with a couple of post-graduate degrees and diplomas in leadership and management.

My current job as a dementia and wellbeing lead involves leading and supporting team members, as well as learning how to best support people living with dementia. This is about treating each person as a unique individual, enjoying health, dignity, participation and social inclusion, as well as taking into consideration the culture, spirituality and religious sentiments of each individual. So it's about finding creative ways to communicate and bringing a holistic input towards the person's wellbeing while co-producing care outcomes together with the person living with dementia.

I also volunteer with the Alzheimer's Society as a dementia friends' champion. I think that being from India, I can look at treating the disease from a different perspective, and I help raise awareness among ethnic minority communities. For example, a person with dementia may revert back to their own first language, so it can be helpful having someone with a similar ethnic background with them, so they don't feel uncomfortable. I can also have fluent conversations in different languages and incorporate our cultural elements into my conversation to get in touch with the real person inside the body. I ran a dementia friends' session in English with a Chinese interpreter taking and interpreting questions, so language is not a barrier if you want to make a difference.

Versha at a cultural event for the Hindu Cultural Association, 2018

I also volunteer with a local group called the Hindu Cultural Association as a governor and executive member. I help fundraise and organise cultural events and work in partnership with museums to celebrate Indian festivals. I also support many children learning Indian Bollywood dancing so they can keep in touch with their roots and where their parents are from.

Versha pictured with her colleagues receiving a Small Workforce Healthcare Award at Swansea Stadium, 2015

I'm hoping to have my own charity one day to pay for the education of underprivileged children in places like Africa and India and to create volunteer groups that will make a difference to people there. I would also like to create some scholarship opportunities here. After I lost my dad, I couldn't afford my studies for a long time and had to work full time and study via distance learning. It was incredibly challenging, but I was highly driven. I would want to support other hardworking pupils with a similar drive and passion and to at least take away the financial impediment depriving them of the education they may deserve.

I also want to work in some way related to autism and dementia. My sister-in-law is a child specialist back home in India and wants to help kids at school with dyslexia, so we'll probably run the charity together in some way. Currently, I'm a community governor of a public high school and a trustee of Women's Aid. I really wish that there were 48 hours in a day to achieve what I want to achieve in my life, to be of help to people and to actually make a genuine difference. It's easier said than done, but it's very rewarding.

I feel now that I am neither Indian nor Welsh, but a blend of the two incredible cultures. I'm proud to be the daughter of my parents and wife of my husband and also to be an individual who has an opinion and a voice that is heard in the community and is able to make a difference in people's lives. I'm also proud to have won a few awards, including a Welsh Women Achievers' Award, a National Care Award, a Welsh Care Award, Points of Light Awards, and a community service award for ten years from the Hindu Cultural Association. These are all, I think, a recognition of the hard work that anybody would do. Although this was not asked for, it's really nice to be appreciated.

When I won the EMWWAA award in the Self-Development category, I said in my speech that self-development is something that can go on lifelong. I think once you receive an award, you try to better yourself

Versha receiving an EMWWAA Self-Development Award, 2017

every day to live up to the award and what it means to you. For me, it's a reminder to look at how I could improve myself and make a difference to society, which needs a lot of patience and perseverance.

If you genuinely want to make a difference, be part of the community, try and understand the difference that you want to bring from people's perspectives and be part of that change. I think the start is always very small, and then these smaller changes make a bigger difference in time.

I believe that a person who's got passion is already empowered enough to take their passion forward. What I would say from experience is to manage your time well and invest in your passion. Have a person that you look up to and follow their advice, but at the same time, have your own ways of making a difference. Look at the results that you produce, which will guide you in what more you can do.

In order to get to that ultimate goal, it's important that whatever hurdles you may face, especially with regards to your own beliefs and attitudes, you are flexible in challenging yourself and looking at things from a different perspective, to evolve from where you were yesterday and to just keep evolving.

# List of judges

**Professor Julian Sampson**

Julian Sampson is an academic clinical geneticist at the Institute of Medical Genetics, School of Medicine, Cardiff University. He moved to the Institute in 1989 and worked for seven years as an NHS consultant before being appointed Professor of Medical Genetics and, from 2000, Head of Department and Institute. He maintained his clinical practice until 2021, providing clinical services in west Wales and in Cardiff for patients and families affected by rare inherited conditions. The Institute won a Queen's Anniversary Prize for Higher Education in 2007 for its work on inherited diseases. His own research has focussed on the genetic mechanisms, diagnosis and treatment of inherited disease and included the identification of disease-associated genes and the development of accurate genetic tests and novel treatments. In 2002 Julian won funding from the Welsh Government to establish the Wales Gene Park with the aim of 'harnessing genetics and genomics to advance research, healthcare, education and innovation' and he served as its director until 2019. He is a long-serving medical advisor to the Tuberous Sclerosis Association (UK) and scientific advisor to the Tuberous Sclerosis Alliance (USA) and has also served as Chair of the Welsh Scientific Advisory Committee for Welsh Government and on advisory groups for the UK Department of Health and the National Institutes of Health (USA). He is a Fellow of the Academy of Medical Sciences, the Learned Society of Wales and the Royal College of Physicians.

**Sue Essex**

Sue Essex was the first woman Leader of Cardiff City Council. She served as a Member of the newly established National Assembly for Wales for Cardiff North from 1999 to 2007 when she stood down. She was Minister for Environment, Planning and Transport in the first term and then Minister for Finance, Local Government and Public Services in the second term. Since leaving the Assembly Sue has been involved in many current issues including a Review of Affordable Housing in Wales

She is currently Chair of the the voluntary organisation Purple Plaques aiming to get plaques erected celebrating remarkable women in Wales

**Professor Sue Wong**

Professor Susan Wong is currently Professor of Experimental Diabetes and Metabolism at Cardiff University and Honorary Consultant Physician in Diabetes at the University Hospital of Wales, Cardiff. She is a Fellow of the Learned Society of Wales. She has many years of research into the causes of type 1 diabetes, as well as clinical experience in treatment of all aspects of diabetes mellitus. She considers that activities that engage and involve the public understanding scientific research and educating people who do not have a medical or scientific training about medical issues are very important, and integral to her work. She is very keen to address issues of equality, diversity and inclusion and to promote professional development opportunities for all, including women in under-represented communities through mentorship, career advice, and obtaining leadership and management skills within the Welsh higher education and healthcare systems.

**Professor Chris Weedon**

Chris Weedon is Professor Emerita at Cardiff University where she directed the Centre for Critical and Cultural Theory. She has published widely on feminist theory, cultural politics, culture and identity, women's writing, British Black and Asian writing and multi-ethnic Britain. She was involved in Butetown History and Arts Centre for 26 years. She has worked on a range of community-based oral history projects since 1990 with people from various minority communities. Currently, she is also a part of an AHRC-funded research project on refugees in Wales.

In 2010 she announced £4m funding for a project on multiculturalism at Cardiff University that would fund four PhD students, and the research would look at the challenges to culture for both white and Black citizens.

**Professor Terry Threadgold**

Terry Threadgold retired from Cardiff University in 2012 after a long career working in Australia and the UK at the University of Sydney, Monash University and Cardiff University. She was Pro Vice Chancellor Staff and Diversity at Cardiff University from 2008–2012.

In her PVC role she chaired the University Equal Opportunities and Diversity Committee, and the Inclusive Curriculum Steering Group. She was the university equality champion and the senior academic lead on the university's Positive Working Environment, Athena Swan, Investors in People and Stonewall Workplace initiatives, achieving success for the university in all these areas. She was chosen as Stonewall's Welsh workplace champion in 2012. She has an international reputation as a feminist scholar and researcher and for her interdisciplinary work in feminist discourse analysis and critical theory. Her book *Feminist Poetics: Poeisis, Performance, Histories* (Routledge 1997) was a study of race, nation and identity in Australian literature, media and popular culture. Her research on the UK media coverage of asylum and refugee issues between 1999 and 2009 is well known and had considerable impact on Welsh Government policy in these areas. She published *Shoot First and Ask Questions Later: Media Coverage of the 2003 Iraq War* (Peter Lang 2006) with Justin Lewis, Nick Mosdell and Rod Brookes. Her report for Joseph Rowntree, 'Immigration and Inclusion in South Wales' was published in 2008. Since her retirement she has worked as a consultant to more than a dozen universities and as a mentor/coach to senior academic women in the UK and Ireland. She was elected a Fellow of the Learned Society of Wales (LSW) in 2015. As a member of the LSW Council she chaired a Review of Equality, Diversity and Inclusion in the Learned Society (2017–19). She is now Treasurer of the Society and a member of the Executive.

**Mutale Merrill OBE**

Mutale Merrill is the founding Chief Executive of Bawso, a leading third sector provider for BME women and children facing domestic abuse and all other forms of violence. Mutale has spent many years occupying a number of important roles within the public and voluntary sectors in Wales, including being the first Independent Chair of the Board of Community Health Councils in Wales.

**Julie Morgan MS**

Julie Morgan, Member of the Senedd for Cardiff North, has represented the area for 23 years both as an MP and an MS. Julie has always been a champion of equality and human rights and has been involved in a number of long-running campaigns.

While an MP, Julie presented three Private Members' Bills – one on banning smoking in public places, one on granting votes at 16, and one on preventing under-18s from using sunbeds which became law in 2010. Despite the bill on granting votes at 16 not passing at the time, it paved the way to the voting age being lowered in Wales for devolved Parliament and local elections. Julie has also fought for justice for victims of the contaminated blood scandal and successfully lobbied the UK Government to create the Public Inquiry into the scandal which is currently ongoing.

In the Senedd, Julie chaired Cross-Party Groups on Cancer, Gypsies and Travellers, PCS Union, Haemophilia and Contaminated Blood, and Children until December 2018 when she was appointed as Deputy Minister for Health and Social Services in Mark Drakeford's new government. Julie remains in Mark Drakeford's cabinet as Deputy Minister for Social Services following the 2021 Senedd elections. As Deputy Minister, Julie has set up a pilot for Baby Bundles and brought into law the removal of the defence of reasonable punishment.

Julie was a founder member of the Welsh Refugee Council. She was also a founder member of the Women's Arts Association; and has been a patron of the Touch Trust, Advocacy Matters, Pontyclun Bosom Pals and Women Seeking Sanctuary Advocacy Group Wales. Julie is also a trustee of Life for African Mothers and Vice President of City Hospice.

**Professor Radhika Mohanram**

Radhika Mohanram was born and raised in India and is Professor of Postcolonial Studies in the School of English, Communication and Philosophy in Cardiff University. She is currently working on two different projects: 1) a funded project on collecting life histories of Sri Lankan Tamil and Syrian refugees in South Wales and 2) a monograph on how the cultural trauma from the 1947 Indian partition still reverberates in contemporary India.

**Professor Sue Denman**

Professor Sue Denman came to Wales in 2001 to set up the Research Monitoring and Evaluation Unit for the Wales European Funding Office. She remained at the Welsh Government to manage the Wales Office of Research and Development in health and social care, taking over as

Director in 2007. She then joined the staff at the School of Medicine, Cardiff University where she set up the South-East Wales Academic Health Science Partnership. Since retirement Sue has kept in close contact with the University and has undertaken some consultancy work.

**Alison Jackson**
A Glaswegian by birth, Alison Jackson left Scotland soon after graduating in Modern Languages from the University of Glasgow. After switching career path in the 1970s and obtaining a Diploma in Social Work, she worked initially as a Probation Officer and – for the past twenty-five years – as a Family Court Advisor. She has also been involved in various part-time teaching roles, including working in basic education (literacy and numeracy), and teaching social work at Cardiff University.

Alison has always had an international perspective and has been interested in different parts of the world, not just from a linguistic point of view, but also in social-political and cultural terms. She has travelled in Europe, North and South America, Nepal, India, China and Australia, and spent a year as a volunteer with Voluntary Service Overseas teaching in Nigeria.

Identifying herself as a feminist and a socialist, Alison has had a lifelong commitment to campaigning for peace, equality and social justice. Social work has a long tradition of challenging discrimination and inequality of many kinds, trying hard to expose racism, sexism, ageism and other forms of stigma and oppression. Clearly, the struggle is by no means over, as recent events have borne out. EMWWAA has a valuable part to play in this struggle, and Alison has felt honoured to be included. She has found her experiences on the panel of judges inspiring, moving and humbling.

**Dr Stella Diamantidi**
Stella Diamantidi is Associate Dean Student Engagement at Cardiff Metropolitan University since 2019. Her responsibilities include leading on learning, teaching and student engagement initiatives as well as ensuring meaningful student engagement in quality assurance and enhancement. Prior to this role she was Head of Business Dept. with line management responsibilities for large academic teams enabling them to deliver high-quality student-centred provision. She has designed and delivered business and law degrees (QLDs) assessing the achievements of students as well as teaching and learning. She has expertise in external examining, and she is a qualified trainer for the External Examiner Development programme by Advance HE. She chairs a number of Examining Boards; she is a Senior HEA Fellow and a QAA Reviewer for England. She has extensive experience of academic leadership and strategy in higher education, in further education, private provider colleges as well as post-92 Universities.

**Professor Michael Fernando**
Professor Mike Fernando is the Dean of Strategic Development at University of Wales Trinity Saint David. Mike leads on academic development activities across all campuses (Swansea, Carmarthen, Lampeter and London)

and learning centres (Cardiff and Birmingham). Mike oversees strategic projects for the University and aligns them closely with the institutional priorities. Prior to this appointment, Mike served as the Dean of the Faculty of Architecture, Computing and Engineering (FACE). Mike is a Chartered Engineer and an experienced engineering academic, academic consultant for Trans-National Education (TNE) and an industrial consultant for Electromagnetic Compatibility (EMC).

Mike was the first in his family to go to University; he went through the higher education system without having a role model in his family to show him the way. Mike is grateful for all the educators and professionals who supported him through his time studying in higher education. This experience has shaped his perspective on every activity he has been involved with in his HE career to date. Mike leads on the Widening Participation priority for the University; he is passionate about providing equality of opportunity in accessing higher education for all learners, especially those from disadvantaged backgrounds.

**Professor Sheila Hunt**

Professor Sheila is a semi-retired academic with a background in health, nursing, midwifery, and higher education. She now offers education consultancy, personal and leadership coaching and mentorship to organisations dealing with change and individuals building their careers in health, education, government, and the charity sectors.

Her company is – www.sheilahuntcoaching.org

She has held senior leadership positions in Universities in England, Scotland, and Wales and within the NHS and has delivered innovation, change and high-quality service. She has managed a budget of over £20m and provided leadership and motivation to professionally and culturally diverse groups of 400+ staff and over 3,500 students. She understands the value of motivational leadership and how developing a collaborative culture and fostering good relationships can lead to the success of organisations. She values diversity and promotes equality of opportunity and work to ensure these principles are embedded in organisations at all levels. She has an entrepreneurial mindset, combined with a sound business sense and strong communication skills.

**Kully Thiarai**

Kully Thiarai has been Artistic Director and Chief Executive of National Theatre Wales since 2016, during which time she has directed productions including Sisters, *The Stick Maker Tales* and *Tide Whisperer.* Kully has led a number of organisations and companies and was the founding Director of Cast in Doncaster. She is a Clore Theatre Fellow, Fellow of the Royal Society of Arts and a Trustee of the Manchester International Festival. Currently, she is a creative director and CEO of Leeds 2023 – the city's international year of culture.

**Dr Joan Williams**

Consultant in Chemical Pathology and Metabolic Medicine; also held the posts of Postgraduate Organiser, Clinical Director of Pathology, Assessor on various appointments Committees, Inspector for Clinical Pathology Accreditation and completed time at Bro Morgannwg NHS Trust as Deputy Medical Director. Member of Soroptimists International, an advocate of Anti-Human Trafficking Activities with the Wales Anti-Slavery Operational Group raising awareness of this heinous crime and supporting those who support the victims.

**Jane Hutt MS**

Jane is a key figure in the field of social justice in Wales, both in and out of Government. Before she was elected as an Assembly Member she worked in the voluntary sector, campaigned on equalities issues and worked in a range of organisations, as well as serving as a County Councillor for South Glamorgan County Council.

Jane was the first National Co-ordinator of Welsh Women's Aid, providing support services for women and children at risk of domestic abuse and homelessness. The creation of an autonomous Welsh organisation led to the development of a range of refuges and preventative initiatives throughout Wales, including specialist services for young homeless (Llamau), minority ethnic women (BAWSO) and housing and support (Hafan Cymru).

Jane was instrumental in securing funding for one of the first women-only IT training centres in the UK, the Women's Workshop, which provided on-site childcare and targeted women who wanted to return to work. Thousands of women and children benefited from this flagship scheme.

Jane has served as a Minister in the Welsh Government in the portfolios of Health, Social Services, Education and Finance. She is Minister for Social Justice responsible for implementing the Race Equality Action Plan for an Anti Racist Wales.

**Professor Meena Upadhyaya**

Meena Upadhyaya is an honorary distinguished professor in Medical Genetics at Cardiff University, Wales, and honorary Professor at Amrita Institute of Medical Sciences, Kochi, Kerala.

Her research career focused on many genetic disorders, especially neurofibromatosis type I (NF1) and facioscapulohumeral muscular dystrophy (FSHD). She has published over 200 papers and has edited 4 books on NF1 and FSHD. She was awarded the European Theodore Schwann award for her outstanding contributions to NF1 research in 2013, OBE in 2016, and Saint David Award in 2017.

She is a Fellow and Council member for the Learned Society of Wales and the Royal College of Pathologists. She is a Trustee for Nerve Tumours, UK, Race Equality First and Race Council Cymru. She joined the Welsh Government Civil Service Board as a Non-Executive Director in 2020 and the Welsh Government Steering Group for the Race Equality Action Plan in 2021. She also sits on the Advisory Committee of the Purple Plaques and Monumental Welsh Women. Meena is an advocate for promoting equality, diversity, community cohesion, and integration. She is the founder and Chair of the Ethnic Minority Welsh Women Achievement Association (EMWWAA) and the Ethnic Minority Women in Welsh Healthcare (EMWWH).

# About Nazma Ali

The idea of nature being constant as an antidote to the horrors of the world is what binds together the seemingly disparate elements of Nazma Ali's multi-disciplinary art practice. To find her voice, Nazma uses the written word in addition to paint, collage, sculpture, and occasionally performance. Returning to study art at the age of thirty, Nazma won Access Student of the Year Award before going on to gain a Masters Degree in Contemporary Dialogues: Fine Art at Swansea Metropolitan University.

Through her study and art, further informed by cultural traditions and feminism, she aims to capture the spirit of human existence. Nazma was inspired by the 19th century cockle women of Penclawdd bringing their produce to Swansea market, a daily nine-mile each-way journey undertaken on foot, to produce a performative piece, *Lyrical One: Cockles & Mussels* at Mission Gallery in Swansea.

As well as working independently, Nazma has frequently collaborated with fellow artist Mark Stephenson, affording her a Wales–centred but also outward–looking practice, typified by the performance of *Welsh—Asian | Asian—Welsh* at the Senedd in Cardiff under the guise of 'the Glitterationist International'.

The 'Glitterationists' then went on to respond to the theme of the dystopian city in their caricature word-based artwork, *Higher Street*, published by CCQ Magazine (issue 6) and exhibited in Elysium Gallery's *Tales From the Bunker* exhibition. This was a precursor to Nazma and Mark working collaboratively as 'the HigherStreet International' with Swansea's Volcano Theatre on the *From the Station to the Sea* project (re-imagining possibilities for Swansea's High Street as part of the Arts Council of Wales Ideas People Places regeneration programme).

More recently Nazma's practice has shifted to working within the field of wellbeing and she is very much interested in how nature and food can improve emotional health. This was explored in *Artist in Residence: Nazma Botanica* at Swansea's Glynn Vivian Art Gallery, culminating in a large-scale paper-based artwork donated to NHS Wales and from which some of the images featured in this publication are taken.

# Photo credits

**Photo credit: Sian Trenberth**

Hilary Brown, image 5, page 17; Martha Holman, image 6, page 29; Maria Mesa, image 6, page 34; Rachel McDonald, image 2, page 43; Samsunear Ali, image 5, page 50; Poranee James, image 6, page 55; Chetna Sinha, image 4, page 58; Chantal Patel, image 6, page 72; Kamila Hawthorne, image 5, page 93; Kiran Ratna, image 3, page 106; Sarita Pawar, image 5, page 112; Justna Muhith, image 6, page 124; Christina Roy, image 6, page 140; Grace Kerry, image 6, page 157; Sunita Menon, image 3, page 160; Leanne Rahman, image 6, page 170; Humie Webbe, image 6, page 176; Banani Sinha Ray, image 6, page 181; Alka Ahuja, image 6, page 192; Diana De, image 5, page 202; Abi Lasebikan, image 6, page 210; Gaynor Legall, image 6, page 77; Uzo Iwobi, image 6, page 12

**Photo credit: Eve Howard**

Humie Webbe, image 2, page 173

# With thanks